Praise for *52 Weeks to a Sweeter Life for Caregivers, Activists and Helping Professionals*

"I wish this guide had been part of my psychotherapy training's curriculum. *52 Weeks to a Sweeter Life* is an invaluable resource for learning how to take care of yourself while also taking care of others."

SIL HERNANDO
registered psychotherapist
and clinical educator

"Self-care can feel like a monolith, but in *52 Weeks to a Sweeter Life*, Farzana makes it manageable with brief activities that create tangible change in the short-term and leave you reflecting on what's possible for yourself over the longer-term."

JEN VASIC
registered social worker, PhD
candidate, city councillor

"This book has been a lifeline during a period when I felt like I was drowning. It's comprehensive, and the little chunks and offers for deeper dives are really wonderful."

NATASHA STEER
racialized intersectional feminist,
writer and social justice educator

"I've read a number of self-help books and this is the most useful. If I contrast *52 Weeks* to *Atomic Habits*, for example, *52 Weeks* has been much more effective at helping me work through my own personal blocks to self-care."

ZAK GREANT
multi-disciplinary executive with more than twenty-five
years of startup and open source experience

"At long last, here is the guide to self-care and self-healing that healers, activists, and social changemakers have been waiting for. Unpretentious, insightful, and deeply aware of the systemic conditions that influence well-being, psychotherapist and author Farzana Doctor offers down-to-earth advice about personal growth, burnout recovery, and relationship health alongside highly relatable anecdotes from her personal experience. Self-help skeptics and wellness aficionados alike will find grounded, practical wisdom in this succinct yet powerful workbook divided into a series of profoundly helpful themes and exercises. *52 Weeks to a Sweeter Life for Caregivers, Activists and Helping Professionals* should be required reading for anyone who wants to change the world—because as the author reminds us, changing the world requires practicing care for ourselves."

KAI CHENG THOM, MSW, MSC
Certified Professional Life Coach and author
of *Falling Back in Love with Being Human*

52
WEEKS
TO A
SWEETER
LIFE

FOR CAREGIVERS, ACTIVISTS AND HELPING PROFESSIONALS

A Workbook of Emotional Hacks, Self-Care Experiments *and* Other Good Ideas

Douglas & McIntyre

52 WEEKS TO A SWEETER LIFE

FOR CAREGIVERS, ACTIVISTS AND HELPING PROFESSIONALS

FARZANA DOCTOR

Douglas and McIntyre (2013) Ltd.
P.O. Box 219, Madeira Park, BC, V0N 2H0
www.douglas-mcintyre.com

"Boundaries" was first published in *You Still Look the Same*
(Freehand Books, 2022).
Edited by Caroline Skelton
Text and cover design by Setareh Ashrafologhalai
Printed and bound in Canada

Douglas and McIntyre acknowledges the support of the Canada
Council for the Arts, the Government of Canada, and the
Province of British Columbia through the BC Arts Council.

Library and Archives Canada Cataloguing in Publication

Title: 52 weeks to a sweeter life for caregivers, activists and
helping professionals : a workbook of emotional hacks, self-care
experiments and other good ideas / Farzana Doctor.
Other titles: Fifty-two weeks to a sweeter life
for caregivers, activists and helping professionals
Names: Doctor, Farzana, author.
Identifiers: Canadiana (print) 20230594654 | Canadiana
(ebook) 20230594727 | ISBN 9781771624039
(softcover) | ISBN 9781771624046 (EPUB)
Subjects: LCSH: Caregivers—Care—Problems, exercises, etc. |
LCSH: Self-care, Health—Problems, exercises, etc. |
LCGFT: Problems and exercises.
Classification: LCC RA776.95 .D63 2024 | DDC 613.076—dc23

*This book is dedicated to all of you who
make our world kinder, more equitable, socially
just and peaceful. This is sacred work.*

Contents

"Caring for myself is not self-indulgence,
it is self-preservation, and
that is an act of political warfare."

AUDRE LORDE

from "A Burst of Light" © 1988 by
Audre Lorde, Ixia Press, Mineola New York

―――――――――

"I think of therapy, meditation, and other
emotional skill-building as analogous to learning
to swim: It means you have a different relationship
to the water. It doesn't mean that you are to
blame for drowning in a storm. So much of survival
is about who is with you in the waves. And if
you're lucky enough to have access to a boat."

KAI CHENG THOM

from her Instagram account
@kaichengthom

Welcome

THIS BOOK is about self-care and community care.

It's an offering based on the ideas I've picked up over my thirty-five years as a social worker and activist. It's the result of thousands of conversations with friends, clients, colleagues and others, many of whom, like me, have struggled with finding balance. This book explores self-care and community care from an inside-out and collective approach.

This book is for helper and activist types—anyone who works with people and causes—and who has trouble (at least sometimes) putting their own needs first.

Perhaps you are someone who

- provides support to others, in a professional or personal capacity
- does valuable community work, activism or volunteer labour

and

- preaches self-care to others but can't seem to practise it consistently
- supports community care but has trouble asking for help
- is on the edge of burnout or way past that point.

There are so many of us!

TEACHERS, DOCTORS, NURSES, PSYCHOTHERAPISTS, MENTAL HEALTH **WORKERS, DAYCARE PROVIDERS,** PROFESSORS, FAMILY CAREGIVERS, **PERSONAL SUPPORT WORKERS,** LAWYERS, ACTIVISTS, COMMUNITY **LEADERS AND VOLUNTEERS, MASSAGE** THERAPISTS, PHYSIOTHERAPISTS, **HOLISTIC BODY WORKERS, COACHES,** LIBRARY WORKERS, ADVOCATES, **SOCIAL WORKERS, HOSPITAL WORKERS,** SOCIAL SERVICE WORKERS, MIDWIVES, **DOULAS, FIRST RESPONDERS,** SENIOR CARE WORKERS, **OCCUPATIONAL THERAPISTS,** PEER SUPPORT WORKERS, **CHAPLAINS, AND MORE**

How it works:

One quick idea per week

Whether you're super practical or the sort of person who likes to nerd out on information about the nervous system, ask deep questions about childhood or consider socio-political influences, you'll find something interesting and easy to use in each short lesson.

Monthly reflection

Every fourth week is a pause to help you review and reflect on what you learned. Or to catch up on a missed week.

Tips and Deeper Dives

Most weeks include a Tips section with information about how to get the most out of the week's experiment, and some include a Deeper Dive section that will help you find out more. Go to www.farzanadoctor.com/52Weeks to find links for all the websites mentioned in the book. Or, use this handy QR code.

Disclaimer

While the ideas in this book focus on emotional well-being, this book is not intended to be used as a substitute for professional medical or psychological care.

Things I wish I'd been taught when I was ten years old

OUR IDENTITIES, socio-political contexts and histories—and how we learned to adapt to them—are directly connected to how we take care of ourselves and others. You have a history and context that will have impacted how you learned to operate in the world.

That's why I want to start by telling you my story.

Self-care hasn't always been easy for me. It sometimes still isn't.

Growing up, I experienced many blessings and privileges. I had a supportive family and friend circle, and I had access to graduate education. Today, I split my time between writing and a psychotherapy practice. I'm able-bodied and in pretty good health. I have spare time to volunteer for causes I believe in. I haven't had to live through war, famine, natural disasters or poverty.

I've also had my share of struggles. My Indo-Muslim family came to Canada as immigrants, and when I was a kid I experienced a form of gender-based violence called female genital cutting. At school, there was racist bullying. My mother died of cancer when I was eleven. I had to grow up fast.

Doing too much

In my thirties, I worked at a large mental health hospital. There, I managed two addiction programs, facilitated groups and had a caseload of individual clients. I travelled around the province teaching 2SLGBTQ cultural competency to other service providers (oof, this was in the early 2000s and we met a lot of resistance).

There was so much to do, so many gaps to fill. For many personal and structural reasons, I had trouble saying no. The work culture rewarded overwork by piling more on. The bureaucracy was stifling, and one of my direct supervisors was disrespectful. While I loved the clinical work, I didn't yet have a strategy for managing the trauma I was absorbing. It was hard to delegate or ask for help.

At the same time, I was attempting to finish my first novel, which I wrote on weekends or while on "vacation." My inability to rest meant that I was doing too much even during my time off.

I wasn't sleeping well, eating healthily or exercising much. I had no spiritual practice. I considered self-care another to-do on my long and growing list of things I "should" do.

I was great at preaching self-care to my clients, staff and friends, but I rarely made time for it.

After almost a decade of this tedious routine, I quit the job, took on some contract work and started a private practice. I eventually created a writing routine that didn't involve vacation writing. I restarted my own therapy, exercised more, tried meditation. Sometimes I managed it consistently, sometimes not so much. The burnout lifted.

Thanks to community care, I could make these big changes; I'd contemplated them for almost two years, with the help of friends who listened to my repetitive, looping anxieties. My privileges expanded my options: I had enough savings to buffer me while I built my practice because my hospital job paid me more than I needed to pay my bills, and I was in good health with access to universal basic healthcare.

Learning is a process (aka, oops, I did it again)

In my early forties, I began the slow journey into perimenopause, which came with brain fog, fatigue, mood swings and bad sleep. New trauma memories surfaced when I got more involved in FGM/C activism. I was promoting my third novel. My private practice was full. Life had revved up again! I got shingles at age forty-five, which was a huge wake-up call. I had to rest more.

Everything I'd learned about self-care so far was helping me, and yet I was still having a hard time. And so, I made room for spirituality by leaning into guided meditation and reclaiming religious rituals I enjoyed. I returned to therapy, using somatic approaches and parts work to address traumas I'd long been suppressing. I rested more, accepted fewer clients and took mini-breaks from the activism. And once again, in time, I recovered from burnout.

And then came COVID

We all know this story. Most caregivers, community leaders and helping professionals I know were overworking (and for many, this overwork is ongoing). Our clients, patients, families and communities were grappling with more uncertainty, loss, financial instability and chronic stress.

For me, nearly every client session required me to acknowledge and set aside my own COVID anxiety so that I could hold space. One client shared their fears about infection on the same day I was developing a sore throat. Another fumbled with social boundaries the day after I'd clumsily cancelled a family dinner.

By the beginning of 2021, I wasn't quite burnt out, but I was nearing it. I call this "getting crispy"—I was tired, weepy and feeling less generous with clients.

I badly needed a strategy to release the anxiety I was feeling and absorbing. I wanted something body-based and stumbled upon YouTube dance instructors like Tanju and the BMD Crew (yes, go look them up). I followed their routines, sometimes dancing while crying. It wasn't pretty, but it got me through that challenging time.

I learned to dance between sessions or at random moments when I needed it. And just try to stop me when I hear a good song at the grocery store (while my slightly embarrassed partner steers the cart into another aisle).

A ~~work~~ rest in progress: multiple, daily practices

In my early years, my parents were too busy establishing a life in a new country to think about balance. There was some rest during weekends and planned vacations, but I mostly recall my father's twelve-hour workdays and my mother's harried schedule split between housework, parenting and admin at my dad's office. There was a pervasive immigrant mantra of needing to work and study hard (and the message that as racialized people we had to work harder), save money and "get ahead." Tricia Hersey, in her important book *Rest Is Resistance: A Manifesto*, refers to this as "grind culture."

My adult life replicated my childhood experience. It was all about going full steam and waiting to rest on vacations and then wondering why it always felt like not enough time off. Or having a spa day but wishing I could live at the spa. I call this the *grand gesture approach to self-care*. It's reactive, maybe even expensive, and ultimately, not sustainable.

My community care had a similar tone: running headlong into others' crises without checking in on my own capacity. Or having a near breakdown and sending an SOS email to ten friends.

Shortly after my second burnout, I realized—not just intellectually, but in an embodied way—that self-care and community care needed to consist of *multiple*, *daily* practices that regulate my mood and nervous system.

Now—on most days, because nothing is perfect—it looks more like this: scheduling my day with multiple short breaks so there's time to stretch, eat, have a cup of tea, reflect, walk, notice, daydream and have deep thoughts throughout the day.

I go slower, hustle less. If a workday has to be full steam, I create a buffer at the end so I can recover. I reach out to friends more often and about less urgent things. I reach back to offer them the same. I seek mental and physical health care earlier, before things get really bad.

I say "no" more often, respond more slowly to messages, don't overextend as much. This approach feels more grounded and sustainable to me. And I often feel like I have more capacity. It's a work in progress. Or a rest in progress.

It's all structural

While this is my individual story, it's important to emphasize that all of this is *structural*. In other words, socio-political forces play a *major* role in how we're able to survive and thrive in this world. Socio-political factors will also impact our options and choices. For example, not everyone will have the same access to a secure income, affordable daycare, universal healthcare, autonomy and time off, while others will have some or all of these rights and privileges.

Were you raised to be a helper-type?

I know a lot of activists and helper-types. Many of my friends do some kind of direct service work with people. Some are community leaders, activists and volunteers for various organizations and causes. I provide consultation to other counsellors and therapists. On the home front, my partner is a primary caregiver to his elderly mom, who lives with us, and we're lucky to be in the company of many dedicated personal support workers.

What I've learned about activists and helper-types is that most of us were inadvertently *raised* to be in these roles. In other words, the stresses, traumas or losses we experienced growing up and living in an inequitable society *taught* us how to be helpers and activists.

Chances are that most of us took on these helper roles young—in our families, schools and neighbourhoods. We might have been a family mediator, a friend to the bullied, or a do-gooder in our community (I sold Girl Guide cookies, never missed a Halloween UNICEF collection, and was my primary school's crossing guard). Some of these might have been conscious choices; others might have been roles we fell into due to circumstances beyond our control.

The good news: we probably developed superpowers—as empathic listeners, change-makers, crisis managers, social justice warriors or problem-solvers. And maybe we reaped direct rewards (such as praise and accolades) or indirect ones (such as feelings of safety, self-esteem boosts or a sense of purpose) from these superpowers. We learned how to direct our care and love in good ways.

And the bad news? We probably weren't taught how to metabolize messy feelings or manage boundaries. We may consciously or unconsciously believe that we don't deserve care ourselves. We may feel guilty when we take breaks or put ourselves first. We may be running on autopilot, feeling so tired that self-care feels like another to-do on a long list of tasks.

Added on to this are the messages that our inequitable society—and structural forces like colonialism, toxic capitalism, patriarchy, homophobia, transphobia, racism, ableism and ageism—may have offered us about work-life balance and caring for ourselves and others.

Most of us will take care of others before ourselves. We light up during crises and chaos in our organizations, friend groups, families and activist circles, but we can't identify our own impending nervous breakdowns. Self-care is way less exciting than saving the world, right?

I almost titled this book *Things I wish I'd been taught when I was ten years old*. Because what if all of us helper-types had been taught how to balance our care work with taking care of ourselves and each other? My wish for you is that this book will provide a simple path to help explore your own personal and political story around self-care and community care and identify your boundaries and needs.

I hope that all the good energy and love that you bring to the world is balanced with calm, joy and rest. And that your life is ever so sweet.

MONTH
ONE

In these first four weeks, we'll set the context and create a little structure.

WEEK 1

Getting Started

FIRST, LET'S get organized!

Schedule

Put aside 2 minutes per day for reading and pondering the ideas in this book. Set an alarm so you can remember. Or pair this with an established habit, such as your morning coffee, lunch or bedtime routine. Alternatively, you could allocate 10-15 minutes once a week.

Do what's best for you

This book is set up as a weekly, sequential guide. But do what's best for your life! Go at your own pace and in whatever order you'd like. Change is a process, a winding road, not a destination. As circumstances shift, so do our needs.

Play!

Treat this as fun and nurturing self-exploration, not as another task on your to-do list. See this week's Deeper Dive for more on this.

Experiment

Not every strategy will be for you, but it's worth trying them all so you can find your favourites.

Follow your curiosity

Some weeks include suggestions for deeper learning if you're curious to learn more. Otherwise, skip them.

Consider doing this with others

Get a self-care buddy or gather friends for monthly book club conversations. They might help you stick with it, deepen your own understandings and build community. There is a book club meeting guide at the end of this book.

Here's this week's experiment:

I've told you a little about my story. What's yours? Growing up, what were you taught—directly or indirectly—about self-care?

- Think about one of your role models: how do they do self-care? Do they seek out community when they need help?

_____

_____

_____

- What impact does your history, identity and social context play in what you learned about self-care or your ability to practise it?

_____

_____

_____

- What are your perceptions of self-care? Is it a chore on your to-do list, or something pleasurable or fun?

_____

_____

_____

TIPS These reflections can be short or long. Keep them low maintenance. If you find writing daunting, aim for one word or one sentence or simply ponder the questions and skip the writing!

Deeper Dive

Have you heard of Expectancy Theory? First developed by Victor Vroom in 1964, it proposes that when we believe we'll get a desired reward for our efforts, we'll be more motivated to make the effort.

So, if we expect or believe that self-care will be a time-consuming chore or a waste of time, it might become just that, and we might do it less enthusiastically and frequently over time. However, if we perceive self-care to be well-deserved, fun, restful or natural, we might do more of it.

What Exactly Is Self- and Community Care?

What is self-care?

It's personal: Self-care includes activities that take care of our body, mind and spirit. They might include nutrition, pain and illness management, movement, leisure activities, rest, sleep, our home environment, our social lives or our connection with nature and faith. Self-care might include a list of things that we want to say yes to, as well as a list of things that we need to say no to.

It's political: Self-care is about resisting cultural ideas that value work and money over well-being. It's about addressing socio-political barriers to taking care of ourselves and one another.

Its benefits go beyond you: Self-care is contagious. When we look after our own bodies, minds and spirits, we model this care for others. We co-regulate with others who might need calm. We are better equipped to deal with crises, triggers and conflicts amongst us. We have more capacity to love and care for others.

What is community care?

It's action for the collective: Community care values the larger group's well-being. It might look like so many different things: being part of a care team for a sick friend, contributing funds to an art project, growing a community garden, making lunch for your team, providing HEPA air purifiers at indoor events, organizing a book club or joining a protest.

It can be about receiving support too: When we accept care from our community, we participate in it more wholeheartedly. We communicate that giving and receiving care are social norms.

It's also political: Community care calls on us to challenge false and oppressive beliefs that can dehumanize marginalized and vulnerable people. It discourages us from being passive bystanders when we see injustice.

Self-care "versus" community care

In recent years, there has been much valid criticism of self-care and a push towards community care. We've all seen social media posts labelled #SelfCareSunday with images of shopping and pedicures. Now let me be clear: there is nothing wrong with shopping and pedicures, and I'm not here to shame anyone who enjoys these things. But self-care must go beyond individualistic and consumeristic approaches.

Self-care and community care needn't be dichotomous. In my mind, they work together:

- When we include and support one another in self-care, it's also community care.

- Our self-care efforts and their benefits can be contagious, spreading outward to our communities.

- When we view ourselves as part of, and responsible for, a community, the community's well-being and our individual well-being are linked.

    We need a blend of self-care and community care.

Here's this week's experiment:

Reflect on the self-care and community care definitions:

- What do you think of them? What might you add or leave out?

_____

_____

_____

_____

- What are the ways in which self-care and community care intersect or blend in your own life?

Here are examples from my life to get you thinking:

- Sometimes, community care work can be tiring, and I need to shift into some intentional self-care to balance or recover.

- Community care work can be energizing too, and it can fill me with hope, belonging and connection.

- Often, when I connect with my community, I receive support that encourages and reminds me to turn towards self-care.

_____

_____

_____

_____

_____

A REMINDER These reflections are for you. Linger where you feel curious and move on where you don't.

Self-Care and Community Care Assessment
This Is Not a Test

RELAX, YOU won't be graded here. This week focusses on assessing—without judgment—how you're doing.

A little review. Self-care and community care:

- Include deliberate actions to improve or maintain emotional, physical and spiritual well-being on individual and collective levels. They might include a No List of limits and boundaries and will likely include a Yes List of things you want more of in your life, community and the world.

- Are structurally based; socio-political realities will impact our options. For example, not everyone will be able to spend a lot of time or money on self-care or community care, while others will have this privilege.

  Self-care and community care can help us to address our socio-political realities, allowing us to identify issues and respond with greater capacity. With this greater capacity, our collective action may be more harmonious and effective.

Here's this week's experiment:

Check out the example on the next page of a Self- and Community Care Wheel. There are three main sections (physical, emotional and spiritual) in two concentric circles. The inner circle represents self-care and the outer circle community care.

- **Self-care circle:** The physical section includes strategies that support your body's well-being. The emotional strategies section includes strategies that support your mental and emotional health. The spiritual section strategies includes anything that inspires awe and connection to something greater (e.g., faith, religion, nature, humanity).

- **Community care circle:** As above, there are physical, emotional and spiritual sections for the elements of community care that you participate in (both giving and receiving).

Over the week, use the blank wheel (opposite) to fill out your own wheel, noting the activities you actively engage in *in a consistent way* (for example, at least once per week).

- Note that some strategies might fall into both circles, as well as multiple sections. For example, organizing a nature walk with friends might cross emotional, physical and spiritual categories and could be both self-care and community care.

- If you have nothing or very little to write in the sections, don't despair! You picked up this book for a reason. Be patient and kind to yourself.

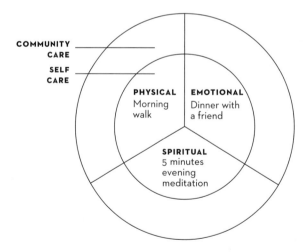

Bookmark this page. You may wish to look back at the wheel seasonally or at the end of the year.

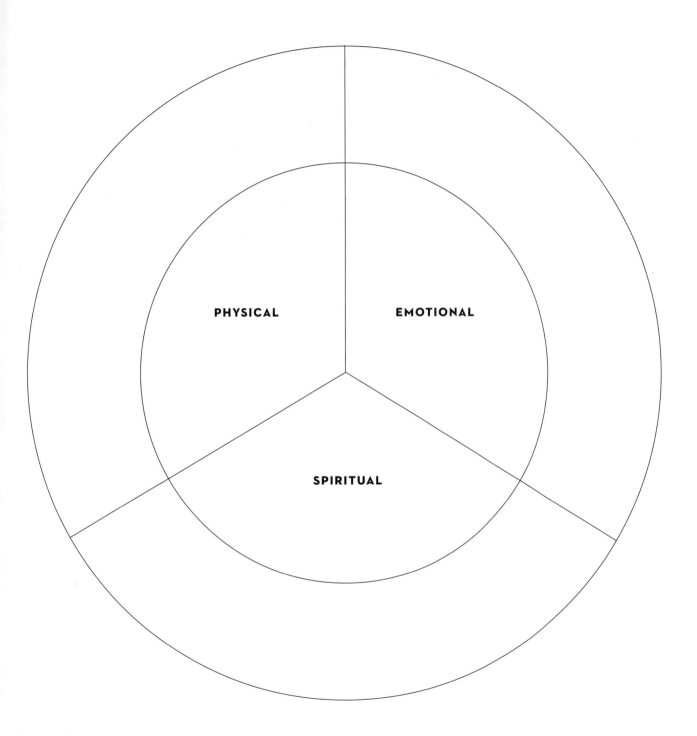

- Now, reflect (non-judgementally!) on what you wrote in your circles on the previous page.

  - What's going well?

  _____

  _____

  _____

  _____

  - Where might you want to develop some new habits and skills?

  _____

  _____

  _____

  _____

TIPS Ask a (compassionate!) loved one to give you some feedback on your assessment. If you're feeling stuck about how to get started, take a look at the examples in Week 5.

WEEK 4
Review and Reflection

CONGRATULATIONS ON completing your first month! These first weeks were about understanding self-care and community care and creating some structure.

Take a few minutes to revisit and absorb this month's content, and to complete or repeat experiments that interested you. Here's a checklist of what we explored in the experiments:

Getting Started

☐ Set up an easy routine to move through this book.

☐ Think about how your role models influenced your self-care beliefs and behaviours.

☐ Consider how your identity, personal history and socio-political factors impact self- and community care.

What Exactly Is Self- and Community Care?

☐ Think about the definitions and whether they make sense for you.

☐ Reflect on the ways in which self-care and community care intersect or blend in your own life.

Self-Care and Community Care Assessment

☐ Complete the wheel.

☐ Be self-compassionate and remember this is a process, a journey.

TIPS I don't know about you, but I sometimes need reminders to keep things simple, and to adjust exercises to suit me.

Here are some different approaches to recording your responses while moving through this workbook:

• If you want, make longer entries.

• If you don't like writing, stick to one word or one sentence.

Don't feel like writing at all? Draw your responses, record your thoughts as voice memos, or use the questions as a conversation guide at your next dinner party, book club meeting or therapy session.

MONTH
TWO

This month, we'll look at habits
and how habit change works—
and why this can feel hard or easy.

WEEK 5

Neuroplasticity Is Cool

WE NOW know that the brain is adaptable—it has an ability to reorganize itself by forming new neural connections. We can "rewire" our brains by strengthening new neural pathways and weakening old ones.

Repetitive acts—both positive and negative—make this rewiring happen. This concept is important for any kind of change we want to make in our lives.

A simple example: I can create a neural pathway by watching *The Mindy Project* in bed until midnight every night (which disrupts my sleep), or I can create a neural pathway by turning off all screens at 9:30 p.m. (which helps my sleep).

A work example: I can strengthen an existing, well-established neural pathway of needlessly rushing to reply to emails in the evening (an anxious habit which disrupts my leisure time), or I can create a new neural pathway by turning off my computer and stopping work at 5:30 p.m.

Understanding neuroplasticity has been helpful in my journey to understand my own behaviour and habits.

Here's this week's experiment:

Reflect on:

• One of your positive habits: how did you build it over time?

_____

_____

_____

- One of your not-so-positive habits: how did you build it over time?

_____

_____

_____

_____

_____

Look back at your Self- and Community Care Wheel and choose one of the habits or skills you identified as an area you would like to grow. Break it down and choose a tiny chunk that you can repeat (more on tiny chunks in Week 7). This will be your neuroplasticity practice.

Some examples of neuroplasticity practice:

LARGER GOAL	TINY CHUNK TO REPEAT
Establish a daily meditation practice	Do a 2-minute meditation at lunchtime, repeating it 3 times this week.
	Ask a friend to join in person or over video conference (to have this cross over into community care).
Establish an exercise routine	Dance to one song, repeating this 3 times a week.
	Do this with an activist group, work team, housemates or family (to have this cross over into community. care).
Become more self-compassionate	Notice one negative thought. Respond to it like your best friend would. Repeat daily.
	Ask your best friend to help you if you get stuck (to have this cross over into community care).

TIPS Asking loved ones, neighbours or co-workers to encourage, remind or join you can make this easier. Remember to be intentional and repetitive. And playful! It doesn't matter how *successful* you are. This is an exercise to learn more about neuroplasticity.

Deeper Dive

See www.farzanadoctor.com/52weeks for a link to a two-minute explainer video on neuroplasticity. For a much deeper dive, check out the book *The Brain That Changes Itself,* by Norman Doidge.

WEEK 6

Change Can Be Hard
Understanding the Homeostatic Impulse

I OFTEN get excited about trying a new wellness habit (Use a lightbox! Sign up for Zumba! Read more! Listen to guided meditation before bed!). But after a couple of weeks... well, I tend to lose interest. I know I'm not alone in this.

It turns out that there is a really good reason why humans have trouble with change: the brain automates to save energy.

Subconscious processes allow us to autopilot things like breathing, digestion, reactions and habits. But the subconscious mind also has an impulse to *keep* us on autopilot, in a comfort zone. This is the homeostatic impulse.

So, when we try new behaviours, thoughts or emotional habits, our subconscious mind will resist, judging the new thing as unfamiliar, uncomfortable and unsafe.

This resistance might be expressed as feelings like the following:

- Apathy ("Why bother using this book? This won't work.")

- Fear ("Oh no! What if I fail, don't do it right or look ridiculous?")

- Physical sensations like aversion or fatigue ("This feels weird" or "I just don't have the energy.")

- General discomfort ("I'd rather be watching *Jane the Virgin*!" That one was me last night when I didn't want to go to bed on time.)

There's an antidote! The way to hack the homeostatic impulse is through *consciousness*. Here are some strategies:

- Mindfully observe the impulse or sensation without judgment, perhaps even with a dose of humour or compassion (more on this in Weeks 26 and 33).

- Set daily intentions or reminders because it's so easy to forget.

- Reduce barriers to doing the new behaviour. For example: by placing the lightbox on my desk so that it's easy to use.

- Make it harder to fall back into old behaviours. For example: removing a television from the bedroom or putting the remote someplace inconvenient.

- Talk about our goals with loved ones and ask for their support.

- Join an IRL or online community for company and mutual aid. For example: I'm currently editing this while engaged in an online #writingsprint (a one-hour time slot where we all agree to write and check in at the end of it).

- Remember the reason why we want to change something.

- Delight in the rewards of small changes (I think most of us forget to do this one).

- Repeat the new behaviour, thought or emotional habit long enough to strengthen the new neural pathway (remember neuroplasticity from last week?).

- Use self-hypnosis to send a new message to the subconscious (more on this in Week 50).

Here's this week's experiment:

- Continue working on the *tiny chunk* you picked in Week 5 (or choose a new one if you prefer). As you do this, notice any reactions driven by the homeostatic impulse. Did you feel apathetic? Afraid? Uncomfortable physical sensations? Did conscious awareness or action help?

_____

_____

_____

_____

_____

_____

_____

_____

TIPS This practice is going to help you when you try out new strategies in the coming months. Reminding myself of the homeostatic impulse made me less impatient and self-judgmental when I was first trying out ideas in this book.

Deeper Dive

Have you heard of the twenty-second rule? We can affect habits by making them either twenty seconds *more convenient* or twenty seconds *less convenient*.

- For example, if I want to stretch more, I could place my yoga mat in a convenient, visible spot. To further reduce the energy and time it takes to get on the mat, I might keep it unrolled.

- On the other hand, if I want to cut back on my doomscrolling, I could put my phone in another room in the evening (a location twenty seconds or more away).

This idea was first developed by author and speaker Shawn Achor. Check out his book *The Happiness Advantage* if you'd like to learn more.

WEEK 7

Tiny Chunks

BY NOW, you're familiar with the concept of tiny chunks (see Week 5). Let's explore this concept a bit more.

Most of us procrastinate when overwhelmed by fear or worry. For many of us, it's the body's freeze response working to protect us. (More about this in Week 13.)

Common thoughts that lead to procrastination are fears of failure, success, humiliation or criticism. We can become mired in perfectionism. When I'm overwhelmed by any of these fears, I lose all my motivation and energy.

If you're having trouble getting started on a task or project, check if the first step is too big or too overwhelming. Breaking it down into tiny chunks can help.

Here are some examples of how I use this concept in my own life:

- When I don't feel like meditating, I'll play a three-minute guided meditation.

- If journaling feels daunting, I'll focus on writing one sentence.

- If I'm having a hard time and need to reach out to someone but have limited capacity, I'll send a very brief text or gif, or forward a reel or meme.

- If I'd like to support a writer colleague's launch but have limited social energy, I might share the info on social media instead, or plan to attend for just a portion of the event.

- When housework feels overwhelming ("adulting" is no fun!), I'll opt to:

- Wash five dishes
- Fold the laundry for the length of one favourite song
- Vacuum for two minutes

And I leave the rest for tomorrow.

I can almost always talk myself into doing something for a few minutes. Then this often inspires a few more minutes—but not always, and that's okay.

Here's this week's experiment:

- Think of one self- or community-care activity that you tend to avoid or that leads you to procrastinate. Be gentle—remember that this is your body's freeze response trying to protect you.

_____

_____

_____

_____

_____

_____

- Play with breaking it down into tiny, imperfect and incomplete chunks. Each chunk should only take a couple of minutes.

_____

_____

_____

_____

_____

_____

_____

_____

- Notice your feelings as you continue to do this over the week. At first you might experience a homeostatic impulse (remember last week?) or hear your inner critic (more on that concept in Week 37). Keep at it.

TIPS Perfectionism is often thought to be a "personality issue." But it's not. It's an adaptation (or a way to solve a problem) to childhood stress and trauma that in adulthood has become unproductive or difficult. If this is a persistent issue for you, consider addressing it through this lens.

One way to interrupt perfectionism is to practise aiming for a B– when attempting a new skill. This can take the pressure off.

Another strategy is to conceptualize perfectionism as an inner critic (more on this in Week 37).

WEEK 8
Review and Reflection

CONGRATULATIONS ON getting to Week 8! This month focussed on understanding aspects of motivation and change.

Take a few minutes to revisit and absorb this month's content, and to complete or repeat experiments that interested you. Here's a checklist of what we explored in the experiments:

Neuroplasticity Is Cool

☐ Reflect on positive and negative habits and how they were built over time.

☐ Use repetition for a self-care or community care goal to better understand neuroplasticity.

Change Can Be Hard

☐ Notice the homeostatic impulse as you work on your goals.

☐ Use conscious awareness as an antidote to the homeostatic impulse.

Tiny Chunks

☐ Break down a self-care or community care goal into tiny chunks to make it easier to accomplish and to interrupt procrastination.

MONTH
THREE

This month, we'll look at societal and individual factors that can lead to overwork and burnout.

WEEK 9

Internalized Capitalism

LET'S SHIFT gears to look at a structural issue—internalized capitalism—that impacts our wellness.

> Internalized capitalism refers to the way we absorb dominant societal norms that value paid work, overwork and the side hustle over health, leisure, rest and relationships. We also learn to value, revere and celebrate those who make more money over those who make less. We learn that we are worthy based on how "productive" we are and much money we "earn."

What's this got to do with self-care and community care? A lot. Internalized capitalism teaches us that individual "productivity" is more important than caring for ourselves, our communities or the planet. It can leave us feeling guilty for not working "enough" and taking time off. It makes us falsely believe that our happiness is based on our income and all the things it can buy us. We can also feel bad when we don't succeed in this unequitable, individualistic system.

Internalized capitalism intersects with all other oppressions, including ableism, classism and ageism. We've seen this on a societal level during the COVID-19 pandemic; there was greater emphasis on reopening the economy than there was on collectivist strategies like paid sick leave or air filtration that would protect everyone—especially those most vulnerable to illness.

Here's a personal example of internalized capitalism:

I am able-bodied and mostly experience good health. However, when I had shingles at forty-five, I had a few months of severe fatigue. I felt like my battery was at 23%; each day I had about three hours of available energy for work or other tasks, and this time was broken up by a need for two daily naps.

Emotionally, I felt low and wondered if getting shingles so young was some kind of personal failure.

I relied on loved ones (with some guilt and awkwardness, because I was not comfortable asking for or receiving help) to walk my dog and help with meals.

I struggled with giving myself time to heal. I booked a week off from my private practice, even though I should have taken a much longer leave of absence, because I worried about income and I didn't want to let clients down. I pushed through, sacrificing my well-being for "productivity."

This was a relatively brief and temporary episode of illness. For those living with chronic illness or physical or mental disabilities, this intersection of internalized capitalism and ableism can be a daily experience.

Many thinkers are now proposing changes to the standard nine-to-five schedule, suggesting that shorter workdays and four-day weeks make us more creative and happy. I imagine that most people, if offered the same income in exchange for fewer hours, would jump at the chance to experiment with this.

Even though more creative and happy employees are also more productive employees (which serves capitalism), shorter days and weeks are not the norm. I think this is because employers (and even some self-employed people) have been indoctrinated with the belief that eight hours and five days is normal and correct and that people who push for shorter workdays or workweeks are "lazy."

We can question and unlearn harmful thinking about capitalism. We can challenge cultural norms that harm us.

Here's this week's experiment:

- How might internalized capitalism impact self- and community care in your life?

- What have you learned about how much work is the "right amount"?

Deeper Dive

Challenging internalized capitalism requires persistent education, unlearning and reflection. I recommend reading books such as *Rest: Why You Get More Done When You Work Less* by Alex Soojung-Kim Pang, *How to Keep House While Drowning* by KC Davis and *Rest is Resistance: A Manifesto* by Tricia Hersey.

Why Is It So Hard to Take Breaks?

AT THE busy hospital where I worked, we were entitled to two fifteen-minute breaks (morning and afternoon) and a half-hour lunch.

I skipped breaks (there's always something to get done, right?) and I nearly always ate my lunch in front of my computer. Same story for most of my co-workers. When I talk to other helping professionals, caregivers or activists, I hear a similar pattern of overwork.

Back then, I saw a naturopath who told me that it was essential to slow down to allow my nervous system to calm. My sympathetic nervous system (more on this next month) was in overdrive. He told me I had the power to manifest a different reality. I rolled my eyes.

Things went downhill from there. That same day, I stayed late at work, to make up for the time "lost" at the naturopath's. Overtired, I went home, was argumentative with my partner and ate popcorn for dinner.

It was hard to change my ways. My obstacles around breaks were:

- **Societal.** Oppression can mean that we work twice as hard for less recognition. Plus, internalized capitalism encourages us to overwork (see last week).

- **Institutional.** The employer gave mixed messages, communicating support for work-life balance but rewarding overwork.

- **Physical**. The more my sympathetic nervous system revved up, the harder it was to slow down (more on this in Week 13). This made it hard for me to calmly reflect on my situation.

- **Skills-based**. I needed to learn to set boundaries (more on this in Week 17).

- **Belief-based**. I thought it was noble to deny my own needs. I couldn't give myself permission to take breaks.

- **Trauma-based**. One of my childhood adaptations to trauma is to over-function. For a long time, I felt like an imposter at my job, so I overcompensated.

- **Vicarious trauma**. I was experiencing a lot of it at that job, which made it difficult to manage my emotions or notice my needs (see Week 11).

- **Emotions-based**. Overworking was a maladaptive way to cope with hard feelings such as fear, despair and helplessness that were triggered by my work and a difficult personal relationship.

> If there's one thing I want you to take from this chapter it's this: our obstacles to self-care are complex!

In the end, it was community care to the rescue. A couple of years after the appointment with the naturopath, a good friend recognized my distress, expressed concern, and urged me to slow down. In a way, she gave me "permission" to take breaks, something I just couldn't offer myself at the time.

I think that our strong attachment (more on this in Week 29) penetrated some of my deeper emotional obstacles to self-care. And I suppose I was ready to hear the message from her then when I hadn't been before.

Today, when I'm feeling confused or anxious about taking a break, I imagine what she would say and *give myself* this "permission." I also routinely offer this reflection to other friends who might need reminders to interrupt their over-functioning or overworking.

You might find that adding more rest to your day is a contagious practice, just as overworking can be. Notice if this is true. It takes a village to challenge internalized capitalism and the other obstacles to self- and community care.

Together, let's bring more gentleness to our days.

Here's this week's experiment:

- Notice if you take breaks during your day. What do you do during them? Are they restful for your mind and body?

_____

_____

_____

_____

_____

_____

- If you don't take breaks, what are your obstacles? Are they external (things that have to do with other people or your environment) or internal (your beliefs, your skills, your body)?

_____

_____

_____

_____

_____

_____

- Address one of these obstacles this week. If it's hard to figure out how, check out the tips at the end of this chapter. Remind (and invite reminders from) co-workers, friends and family to take breaks. Offer one another encouragement and "permission."

_____

_____

_____

_____

_____

TIPS FOR ADDRESSING YOUR OBSTACLES TO TAKING BREAKS

Schedule/automate your breaks

- Set an alarm to help you pause during the day.

- Download an app that reminds you to move periodically, like StretchMinder.

- At the beginning of your day or week, schedule in your breaks or rest just as you'd schedule meetings and tasks. Think of it as making appointments with and for yourself.

- If you can, avoid scheduling meetings or calls fifteen to thirty minutes before your lunch break so that you can complete leftover tasks from the morning, rather than being tempted to do this work during your break. Make your break sacred and work-free.

Do it together

- Create a team self-care basket. A social service team I know keeps one in their shared office. It contains lavender oil, herbal teas, dark chocolate and other snacks. Team members remind one another to use the basket.

- One supervisor I know turns on music at 4 p.m. each day to help everyone "dance it out."

- Ask a buddy to join you for lunch. Talk about non-work things.

- Organize a lunch club. One staff group I knew had a rotating schedule in which each person brought a salad or sweet treat to share with the others.

- Organize a group yoga or meditation session to encourage others to take breaks with you. Sometimes human resources workers can assist in setting up sessions like this.

- During work, volunteer or activist meetings, create a space to talk about self-care and remind one another to take breaks. Schedule times to talk about vicarious trauma and burnout (see Week 11). Encourage your colleagues to work with less urgency and more gentleness.

- If your workplace has a union or wellness committee, get involved.

- For leaders: Discourage overwork through your own behaviour. Don't send or read emails or messages after the end of your workday. Model taking breaks, sick days and vacation time.

Working from home
- Begin and end the day with a ritual that signals a start and a hard stop. For example, you might change clothing or walk around the block (as though travelling to or from work). You might "open" and "close" your office symbolically by turning your computer on or off or putting work items away.

- Do the above for volunteer and activist gigs so that you take a mental break from these too.

- Create an individual self-care basket for your desk (see above).

- Create a space where can you go to get away from your computer, phone or desk.

Breaks for caregivers
- Create a list of two to five people who can be backups for you so that it is easier to take breaks from your care work. For example, we have a neighbour who can drop in to do a quick check on my mother-in-law when there is a gap in care. Another friend can come hang out for two hours.

Deeper Dive

To better understand under-functioning and over-functioning, go to www. farzanadoctor.com/52weeks to listen to Brené Brown's podcast episode on this topic. She also talks about day-to-day anxiety and the contagion of anxiety in groups.

Understanding the Links between Vicarious Trauma and Burnout

I WISH I'd learned about burnout and vicarious trauma when I first engaged in activism and social work practice. It took time for me to understand the impacts of sitting in the pain and oppression of individuals and communities.

Burnout is a state of emotional, physical and mental exhaustion or collapse caused by stress. It can leave us unable to function as we normally would. Vicarious trauma, also known as secondary trauma or compassion fatigue, is the emotional residue we can carry from exposure to other people's pain and trauma stories.

It can accumulate over time and skew the way we view the world.

Vicarious traumatization is a common feature of care and activist work.

Like burnout, we can learn to prevent it, but even more importantly, we need to know how to acknowledge it and address it when it does happen so that we can reduce its impact (and in Weeks 33 and 39, we'll delve deeper into ways to do this).

When I was nineteen, I worked at a shelter for women leaving intimate partner violence. I was a good writer, so one of the tasks I was assigned during night shifts, when the crisis line was quiet, was writing victim-impact letters to expedite housing applications. This involved combing through a woman's intake documents and providing a detailed list of all the forms of violence she'd endured. I absorbed those trauma stories—how could I not?

As I continued to work in the field, I grew increasingly hypervigilant to violence and I couldn't stop thinking about my clients even when off shift. This was vicarious trauma.

With each of my subsequent jobs, I pushed back against this distress by changing employers, thinking that "a change is as good as a rest." But without the skills to manage vicarious trauma, I wasn't finding true relief. And then I burned out, and while there were other factors that contributed to the burnout, vicarious trauma was a main one. It would be many years before I learned how to identify and release vicarious trauma, and later, how to protect myself from it.

The same went for my activist work. We don't often associate vicarious trauma with activist and community work, but all care work can expose us to individual and collective trauma. Besides that, social change can feel slow, yet the issues we're addressing are urgent and often overwhelming.

I found myself taking a similar approach—quitting and joining a new cause—to cope with the helplessness and exposure to pain. Some of these work environments and activist groups were oppressive: there were messy fights and power struggles. I likely contributed to these cultures with my own reactivity. I am sure that sometimes I encouraged overwork and overlooked self- and community care.

Without the awareness, skills and supports to cope with vicarious traumatization, it was hard to make sense of my experience. But now I can. Here's the "math" of vicarious trauma and burnout for me:

Exposure to emotional pain and oppression
- self- and community care
- being able to ask for help
- boundaries with time and energy
- nurturing environment
- group or organizational supports
= vicarious trauma and burnout

But also, the opposite can be true.

Exposure to emotional pain and oppression
+ self- and community care
+ asking for help
+ boundaries with time and energy
+ nurturing environment
+ group or organizational supports
= more balanced, sustainable and joyful work

Here's this week's experiment:

- Reflect on a past experience of vicarious traumatization in your care or activist work. How did you identify it? How did you manage it? Did others support you in this?

_____

_____

_____

_____

_____

- Review a time in your life when you felt burnt out, or close to burnout. What factors got you there?

_____

_____

_____

_____

_____

- Review a time in your life when there was balance. What factors got you there?

_____

_____

_____

_____

_____

- How might you help yourself pay attention to your personal "math" around vicarious trauma and burnout?

_____

_____

_____

_____

_____

- How might you contribute positively to the groups that you're a part of so that there is more emphasis on self- and community care?

_____

_____

_____

_____

_____

AN IMPORTANT CAVEAT ABOUT HARMFUL WORKPLACES, ORGANIZATIONS OR GROUPS:

If your burnout is primarily caused by a harmful context (for example, where there is a lack of emotional or physical safety, overwork, micromanagement, toxic relationships, or you are not valued), the solution doesn't lie in taking better care of yourself. The problem is the workplace, organization or group.

However, self- and community care can be worthwhile balms and Band-Aids. They help you cope, get clarity, rest and recover while you sort out what to do next. They might increase your capacity to join forces with others to influence or demand changes.

If you are in a position of influence or power at your workplace, organization or activist group, you can use the ideas in this book to reduce overwork and create a more nurturing context.

WEEK 12

Review and Reflection

CONGRATS ON getting to Week 12! You're three months—an entire season—into this process! In addition to reviewing the past three weeks, you might find it interesting to do a quick quarterly review of the Self- and Community Care Wheel (Week 3). Has anything changed in the past three months?

Take a few minutes to revisit and absorb this month's content, and to complete or repeat experiments that interested you. Here's a checklist of what we explored in the experiments:

Internalized Capitalism

☐ Think about how internalized capitalism impacts self- and community care in your life.

☐ Reflect on time off and how much work is the right amount.

Why Is It So Hard to Take Breaks?

☐ Notice if you take breaks during your day, what you do during them, and whether they are restful for your mind and body.

☐ If you don't take breaks, identify your obstacles.

Understanding the Links between Vicarious Trauma and Burnout

☐ Reflect on experiences of vicarious traumatization, burnout and balance in your care or activist work.

☐ Consider how you might help yourself pay attention to your personal "math" around vicarious trauma and burnout.

☐ Identify how you might contribute positively to the groups that you're a part of so that there is more emphasis on self- and community care.

MONTH
FOUR

This month, our focus is on stress
and the nervous system, and their
links to self- and community care.

WEEK 13
Completing the Stress Response Cycle

FOR ME, a big part of self-care is finding ways to regulate my nervous system. And because we co-regulate with those around us, nervous system care can translate into community care.

But first, a little review of how our stress response system works. When we're triggered by a stressful event, part of our brain, including the amygdala, signals a stress response. For example, when I have to give a speech, my palms sweat, my hands tremble, my heart races and I need to have a last-minute pee. I want to get out of there.

Even though the stress trigger (the speech) isn't life-threatening, my body reacts as though I am being chased by a lion.

In this example, I'm having a flight response. Other responses to threat might be to get agitated or angry (a fight response), being unable to speak or move (a freeze response), appeasing behaviour to try to get out of the situation (a fawn response) or feeling sleepy or dissociative (a collapse and play dead response).

If I *was* being chased by lions, these stress responses would be terrific. I *would* need to fight or flee or freeze or fawn or play dead. If I survived the attack, I might seek safety and then rest. There would be a *beginning*, *middle* and *end* to the stress cycle.

What happens instead is that I experience all those stress symptoms from the speech (or interpersonal conflict, or microaggression, or getting cut off in traffic, or any other modern-day situation) and I get *stuck* in the beginning stage of stress response and can't complete the cycle because it's socially inappropriate or unsafe to do so. I couldn't, for instance, run screaming from the room. Also, a part of my brain knows that it's somewhat safe to carry on.

In this situation, the energy of flight gets stuck in my body. I don't experience the release that comes from the middle and end of the stress response cycle. If this happens chronically, there can be physiological consequences, including illness (see Week 34's Deeper Dive).

In their book *Burnout: The Secret to Unlocking the Stress Cycle*, authors Amelia and Emily Nagoski encourage us to *complete the cycle* with a burst of physical activity (a release of energy), seeking safety through the support of a loved one (they suggest an oxytocin-releasing twenty-second hug with a trusted human or pet) and then resting with a nap or longer sleep. Other strategies include tensing and releasing all your muscles for ten seconds, laughing, crying and creative expression.

So back to my speech: five minutes before, I need to do some long exhalations to resource myself somatically (see Week 15). After, I might have to release any stuck energy by dancing it out, or tensing and releasing, or starting a pillow fight (just checking to see if you're still with me after this super long explanation).

I find it helpful to complete the stress response cycle many times each day: after intense client sessions, for example, or difficult activist meetings, or even after holding space for a friend who is going through a hard time. The ways in which our brains register threat and our bodies hold tension can be subtle and hard to identify, so frequent nervous system support is useful.

Here's this week's experiment:

- Think about a recent, everyday stress event (for example, a microaggression, a conflict or anything that frightened you). What happened next with the stress? Did the stress get "stuck"?

- At least three times this week, attempt to complete the stress response cycle with a burst of physical activity, tensing and releasing muscles for ten seconds, finding social support or a hug, or using laughter, crying, creative expression or rest. What did you notice?

_____

_____

_____

_____

- Remind and invite reminders from loved ones to complete the stress response cycle. When we are stuck in stress, we can sometimes forget to do this. My partner will notice when I am glassy-eyed and ask me what's wrong. This will cue me to do a quick internal check about my Window of Capacity (more on this next week) or unreleased fight or flight energy.

- Something fun: observe other animals as they complete the stress response cycle. For example, dogs will often "shake off" energy after minor stressors like being petted by a stranger.

TIPS Exercise and movement can be fraught for many of us. We'll delve into body-neutral and joyful ways to get that physical burst in Week 35.

Deeper Dive

See www.farzanadoctor.com/52weeks for a short video that describes the stress responses fight, flight, freeze and fawn.

WEEK 14

Nervous System Care

LET'S CONTINUE with stress and the nervous system.

One model for understanding the nervous system is the Window of Tolerance, developed by Dan Siegel. It describes an optimal state of stimulation in which we function well and feel grounded, safe and socially engaged.

Some practitioners—Linda Thai, for example—prefer the term Window of Capacity because "tolerance" suggests the need to push through or tolerate, which echoes internalized capitalism and ableism, while "capacity" emphasizes noticing how resourced we feel. A more colloquial way to express this is "bandwidth."

There are three main states in this model. I like to visualize this as a house:

- The main part of the house is the Window of Capacity, where we feel safe, calm and socially engaged.

- The attic is a zone of hyper-arousal, where we might feel reactive, anxious and unsettled, with an urge to fight, flee or freeze. We are about to "go through the roof."

- The basement is the zone of hypo-arousal, where we may get numb or stuck, feel the need to placate, or be dissociative (the freeze, fawn or collapse stress responses). We are in a dark space.

When we are stressed or our nervous system perceives threat, we have *automatic* and *lightning-quick* responses that take us out of the Window of Capacity and into hyper-arousal and hypo-arousal.

I've noticed that people can feel immense shame when they experience these shifts. But there's no shame in our fight, flight, freeze, fawn, collapse

responses. Our goal is to notice the shifts as they are happening and then support our minds and bodies to gently return to the Window of Capacity.

Another important thing to know about the Window of Capacity: stress and trauma will narrow or shrink it (visualize the main floor of the house having a much lower ceiling and higher floor), and as a result we'll feel more easily dysregulated. Trauma can be viewed broadly to include episodes of overwhelming fear and harm in childhood and adulthood as well as daily experiences of microaggressions and oppression. Also consider that vicarious trauma (see Week 11) can shrink the Window of Capacity.

We can expand our Window of Capacity with self-care, community care and somatic hacks (see Week 15).

Tune in to the Window of Capacity

I know I'm in my Window of Capacity when I feel compassion, curiosity and calm toward myself and others.

I know I'm close to or within hyper-arousal when I get cranky at the drop of a hat. In those moments my heart pounds, I get sweaty and I lose my appetite.

I know I'm close to or within hypo-arousal when I feel spacey or shut down. I might numb out in front of the TV or dissociate.

If I'm noticing hyper-arousal or hypo-arousal while working with people or causes, I might take a moment to check in with myself and assess whether I have been impacted by vicarious trauma or am nearing burnout (see Week 11).

What do these states feel and look like for you?

Here's this week's experiment:

- Take a minute to notice your state of arousal right now. Which "part of the house" are you in?

- Consider taking ten seconds each day to notice your state of arousal. You might stack this onto an already established habit, such as brushing your teeth or eating your lunch or turning on your computer, so that it's easier to remember. Next week, we'll take this activity one step further.

- Remind and invite reminders from loved ones, co-workers or activist buddies to do this state of arousal check-in. It's a great way to start a meeting or shift.

Deeper Dive

- See www.farzanadoctor.com/52weeks for a Window of Tolerance infographic from the National Institute for the Clinical Application of Behavioural Medicine (NICABM).

- If you're interested in learning more about this model, see www.farzanadoctor.com/52weeks for a link to an affordable course offered by mental health clinician and educator Linda Thai. This course is available to both professionals and non-professionals. I took it in 2021 and found it personally and professionally helpful.

Somatic Hacks

DID YOU notice your Window of Capacity last week? Were there times that you felt spikes to hyper-arousal or drops to hypo-arousal?

Were there times during the week when the window shrunk or expanded?

Remember that these shifts in our nervous system are *expected* and *normal* because our stress levels and resources fluctuate. Most of us have been unfairly shamed for our stress and trauma responses and have internalized the shame. This adds a burden of suffering to these already challenging fluctuations.

It's useful to become aware of what impacts your nervous system. I've noticed that sleep is a resource that influences mine in a big way. I slept poorly last week, and I was more reactive (hyper-aroused, in the attic, going through the roof) to irritations, like nearby construction noise, that would normally slide off my back. On the other hand, I slept well this week, and I remained steady (in my Window of Capacity, sitting comfortably in the house) when I received upsetting news (a relative in the hospital).

Other stressors that can impact my window's capacity are interpersonal conflicts (arguments with my partner), hormonal changes (ooof, perimenopause), not enough alone time (why did I overschedule myself?) and low blood sugar.

When we notice these shifts happening, we can use body-based strategies to help us. We can *downregulate* (if we're hyper-aroused) or *upregulate* (if hypo-aroused). Another way to imagine this is helping ourselves "go downstairs" or "come upstairs."

Here are my favourite downregulating techniques for hyper-arousal:

- Releasing energy with ten jumping jacks, dancing, shaking my arms and legs

- Breathing through my nose and ensuring my exhalations are longer than my inhalations

- Rocking from side to side or tossing a ball from one hand to another (an example of bilateral stimulation—see Deeper Dive)

- Listening to autonomous sensory meridian response (ASMR) recordings or guided meditations

- Cuddling a dog or my partner

Here are my favourite upregulating techniques for hypo-arousal:

- Orienting or "coming back" to the room by moving the head and body (not just the eyes) and noticing lots of details and colours

- Humming, singing, yelling or making other sounds (a good counter to the nervous system's collapse response)

- Feeling an object with lots of texture

- Movement like stomping feet and stretching arms

- Thymus thump—lightly tapping or thumping the middle of the chest

Each of us is unique, with different nervous systems and responses, so experiment to find your favourite upregulating and downregulating techniques. There are thousands of ways to do this.

Many of these strategies are subtle enough that they can be used in meetings or in public. For example: if I'm feeling triggered during an activist meeting, or if I'm reacting to a client's traumatic material, I'll very intentionally regulate my breathing or rock gently from side to side. I've noticed that whenever I do this, there is a palpable impact on those around me. Our self-regulation is contagious. Our self-care can be community care.

Here's this week's experiment:

- What resources and stressors impact your Window of Capacity?

_____

_____

_____

_____

_____

- Brainstorm strategies that help you to downregulate ("go downstairs") or upregulate ("come upstairs").

_____

_____

_____

_____

_____

Deeper Dive

Bilateral stimulation (BLS) was discovered by Francine Shapiro, the developer of Eye Movement Desensitization and Reprocessing (EMDR). BLS activates both sides of the brain in a rhythmic left-right pattern. It can be visual (moving the eyes), auditory (sounds that move from one ear to the other), tactile (tapping alternating parts of the body) or movement (such as passing an object from one hand to the other, walking, swaying).

A 2018 study of 1,109 subjects, published in the _Journal of Biotechnology and Biomedical Science_, used bilateral alternating stimulation in tactile form, and showed a statistically significant reduction in levels of emotional and physical distress.

We can use bilateral stimulation to decrease our own overwhelm and feel less stuck in distressing thoughts and emotions.

Review and Reflection

WHAT? WE'RE already at the four-month mark and one-third of the way through the year!

This month we focussed on understanding the nervous system.

Take a few minutes to revisit and absorb this month's content, and to complete or repeat experiments that interested you. Here's a checklist of what we explored in the experiments:

Completing the Stress Response Cycle

☐ Understand how the stress response works.

☐ Try out strategies to complete the stress response cycle.

Nervous System Care

☐ Learn about the Window of Capacity, hyper-arousal and hypo-arousal.

☐ Notice the shifts in your "house."

Somatic Hacks

☐ Use somatic strategies to downregulate or upregulate in order to return to your Window of Capacity.

A REMINDER Use these review weeks to look over the material from the previous weeks, reflect on what worked, and *remain curious* about this process. You can also use this week to catch up on exercises or repeat activities that were especially interesting to you. Keep it simple and low-maintenance.

MONTH
FIVE

This month, we'll take a look
at boundaries and their link to
self- and community care.

What We Learned about Boundaries

MOST HELPER-TYPES and activists tell me that sorting out boundaries is complicated for them. I know it is for me.

In a nutshell, boundaries are about what's okay (and not okay) in terms of:

- Your capacity (your energy, time, skills, abilities, your nervous system's state) and

- Your relationship (your role, closeness, connection) to the other person

Examples of boundaries that we need for self-care can include:

- Our ability to take breaks and rest (see Week 10)

- Saying no or setting limits in response to a request

- Limiting the amount of time you spend doing care work or activism

- Letting someone know you don't like something

- Resisting internalized capitalism and ableism (see Week 9)

- Taking a break from our phones, emails and online life (Week 47)

- Taking time to prevent or reduce the impact of vicarious trauma (Weeks 11, 33 and 39)

- Interrupting over-functioning (Weeks 10 and 49)

For me, boundaries can feel slippery because each situation and relationship is unique, demanding a new (or newly considered) response.

Sometimes my boundaries can feel too rigid—like rules that don't feel generous enough. And then sometimes my boundaries are too loose, and I can end up feeling resentful and tired.

For years, I wasn't aware of the childhood influences that led to difficulties with boundaries. I needed therapists and friends to point them out to me.

EXAMPLES OF CHILDHOOD INFLUENCES THAT IMPACT OUR BOUNDARIES

- If your boundaries were routinely violated due to abuse or neglect or oppression

- If your caregivers were not well-resourced and you had to be a child mediator, caregiver or language interpreter (also known as a parentified child)

- If you had to people-please or code-switch to avoid negative reactions or consequences from others

- If you were socialized feminine and societal expectations (from media, religion, family, school) encouraged you to put others' needs before your own

- If you are a highly sensitive person or an empath, and this trait wasn't honoured, or worse, it was ridiculed (see Week 19)

Here's this week's experiment:

- Jot down your reactions to the childhood influences listed in the box above. What struck a chord? What might you add to the list?

_____

_____

_____

_____

- Flip back to Week 1 and your memories of what you learned about self-care and community care growing up. Consider the role that boundaries (or their violations) may have played in your perceptions about self- and community care.

_____

_____

_____

_____

_____

Don't worry! We'll look at tools for creating boundaries next week.

TIPS Speak to a trusted loved one (perhaps someone who's known you a long time) or a professional who can give you feedback and support about your tendencies around boundaries.

WEEK 18
Creating Boundaries

NOW THAT we have a sense of our tendencies around boundaries, how do we create them?

A reminder: boundaries are about what's okay (and not okay) based on your capacity and your relationship to the other person.

Here are some examples for thinking this through:

I recently received a workshop request from an organization. Their email was vague and didn't include information about learning goals or payment.

Capacity: Do the learning goals fit with my skills and schedule? What's the payment?

Relationship: When information isn't provided up front, I don't feel good about it.

My answer: I'll ask the questions, wait for the reply and then assess.

A non-binary friend would like me to accompany them to a morning doctor's appointment. I'll be there to offer allyship as a cisgender person. They want witnessing and for me to take notes. After, we'll have coffee and debrief.

Capacity: The only boundary is time-oriented—I have a meeting at noon and will need to get home before that. The request is super clear and within my abilities and energy.

Relationship: I trust my friend's ability to communicate their needs to me and I'm glad they trust me enough to ask for this care. Plus, my friend is respectful of my time and it's fun to hang out with them.

My answer: An enthusiastic yes!

> I have been asked to speak on a panel. It's been a busy month with this particular activist group because we are in the middle of a campaign. I feel mixed—I am committed to the work but also tired.

Capacity: When I'm confused, I trust my body to help me set the boundary. Do I have adequate energy for this task? Is my body resourced enough (have I been able to get enough rest, exercise, good food, etc.) and am I consistently returning to my Window of Capacity (Week 14)? My hunch is that I'm not.

Relationship: I like my activist buddies and would like to stretch to say yes. However, if I say yes to them when I'm not resourced enough, I might feel burnt out or resentful. That's not good for our relationship. My well-being must come first.

My answer: Looks like it has to be a no from me.

If you are a professional helper, include your *scope of practice* when considering your capacity and your *professional boundaries* when considering the relationship.

Here's an example:

> A client has asked me to attend his graduation and a post-ceremony celebration dinner. He says that our work over the past four years, which included supporting him to cope with multiple academic stressors, was helpful in successfully reaching this milestone.

Capacity: While it's not directly in my scope of practice to do either of the requests, I check in with colleagues and we discuss the potential positive and negative consequences for the client. The date, time and location work for me to attend the short ceremony.

Relationship: Attending the ceremony is a grey area and permissible. It's against my professional boundaries to attend the social event after the graduation.

My answer: After reviewing the potential positive and negative consequences with the client, we agree that I will attend for thirty minutes then leave. After, we'll debrief about any issues or feelings that arose from the ceremony and my presence.

Here's this week's experiment:

- Consider recent requests you have received from co-workers, clients, friends, activist buddies, family members or community groups. Pick one that feels simple and another that is murkier and requires more consideration. Decide what's okay (and not okay) based on your capacity and the relationship.

_____

_____

_____

_____

_____

_____

_____

_____

- If you are new at practising boundary setting, you may find that some people in your life will be confused by, or unhappy with, new boundaries. Notice your reactions to others' feelings.

_____

_____

_____

_____

_____

TIPS If you're having trouble, do a "gut check." When the boundary question first came up, what was your immediate gut reaction? Queasiness is often my clue that I need to *slow down*, ponder my feelings and boundaries or consult with a friend or colleague before responding to the request.

WEEK 19

Protecting Your Energy and Boundaries with Imagery

HAVE YOU ever been in conversation with someone and become inexplicably fatigued? Many people—especially those who are highly sensitive, or empathic—can absorb others' energies and emotions without being aware of it.

This concept is impossible to objectively measure, so keep an open mind and notice your own experiences.

When I first learned about what it means to be a highly sensitive person, I had an aha moment: I realized that when I'm around people, I needed to learn how to decipher which feelings were mine and which were not. I use many of the following techniques to ground myself and to maintain boundaries.

- **The Energy Loop**: This strategy helps you to symbolically remember that you don't have to take on another's emotions. I find it helps me to hold space more easily (see Week 31 for more on this): when in conversation with someone, imagine a loop forming and flowing between you so that the other person's energy circulates back to them.

- **The Energy Zip-up**: This popular energy psychology technique uses a visualization of sealing your body's energy before you go out or meet with people. Here's how it works: as though zipping up a parka, make an upward motion from your pelvic bone up to your lower lip. Then make a motion of locking the zipper and putting away or throwing away the key.

- **The Light Bubble**: Visualize a protective, light-filled bubble around you that keeps your own energy separate from others'.

- **Clearing:** If you feel you did pick up others' energies and emotions, you can imagine sending back anything that doesn't belong to you. I like to do it with love, humour and imagery: a return-to-sender package, or cutting a cord that might have attached. A colleague imagines "dusting themselves off." If you have a spiritual practice, ask for support to return or clear others' energies.

- **Nature:** I try to spend time in nature, especially if I feel depleted by others' energies. I go to a local park or walk by the lake. One explanation for why this is calming is that negative ions produced by moving water and plants are believed to improve psychological well-being. A 2018 review of ionization studies in the *International Journal of Molecular Science* found that negative ions could regulate sleep and mood and reduce stress.

Here's this week's experiment:

- Notice when you feel impacted by someone else's energy and emotions. Go into a room of strangers or pay attention to the subtle shifts you feel when among loved ones, co-workers or friends.

- Test out one or more of the above techniques for protecting your energetic boundaries or for clearing your energy.

Deeper Dive

- Psychologist Elaine Aron coined the term Highly Sensitive Person, or HSP. She posits that about 15–20% of the population are HSPs who are more tuned in to people's feelings, as well as other stimuli such as noise, smells and light. They may be more empathetic and more bothered than other people by violence. HSPs tend to gravitate towards the arts and helping professions. See www.farzanadoctor.com/52weeks for a link to a self-test.

- If you think you might be an HSP, check out Judith Orloff's book *The Empath's Survival Guide: Life Strategies for Sensitive People*. It offers insights about managing your energy and relationships.

WEEK 20

Review and Reflection

MONTH FIVE was all about boundaries, an essential topic for everyone, and especially caregivers, activists and helping professionals.

Take a few minutes to revisit and absorb this month's content, and to complete or repeat experiments that interested you. Here's a checklist of what we explored in the experiments:

What We Learned about Boundaries

☐ Reflect on childhood experiences that may have influenced how you approach boundaries.

☐ Flip back to Week 1 and what you learned about self-care and community care growing up. Consider the role that boundaries may have played in your perceptions about self-care.

Creating Boundaries

☐ Consider recent requests you have received and practise setting boundaries based on your capacity and the relationship.

☐ Notice your reactions to others' feelings when you set new boundaries.

Protecting Your Energy and Boundaries with Imagery

☐ Notice when you feel impacted by another's energy and emotions.

☐ Test out one or more of the techniques for protecting your energetic boundaries or for clearing your energy.

Below is a poem from *You Still Look the Same,* a poetry collection I wrote in my forties. This was a time of change and growth for me, and I did a lot of thinking about boundaries.

Boundaries

yours are tensor bandages
stretchy yet firm
holding you in
keeping tendons warm
injuries protected

mine are band-aids
from back of drawer
never the right size
adhesive dried up
they slip off
at awkward moments

I wish sometimes
especially when
—or perhaps before—
I skinned a knee
sprained an ankle
I had your first-aid kit

MONTH
SIX

This month, we return to discussions
about motivation and habits and how they
apply to self-care and community care.

If you'd like a review of what we've covered
on this topic so far, glance back at Weeks 5–7.

Learn about Your Motivation Tendency

BY NOW you've probably noticed how your motivation rises and falls through some of the self-care experiments. Perhaps you've even lost some momentum while moving through this book. Here's one tool for understanding why this happens.

Gretchen Rubin, author of *The Four Tendencies*, studies motivation and how we respond to internal and external expectations. She posits that we have a dominant "tendency," which she labels as: Upholder, Questioner, Obliger or Rebel. Some of us have a *combination* of tendencies, rather than one dominant one.

Gretchen Rubin's theory in a nutshell

- Upholders tend to be motivated by internal and external expectations. They tend to value self-created goals and external accountability.

- Questioners tend to be more motivated by internal expectations, but not external ones. They tend to value research-based rationales for the goal.

- Obligers tend to be more motivated by external expectations, but not internal ones. They tend to value teamwork and external accountability.

- Rebels tend to not be motivated by any expectations and resist them. They tend to value autonomous choice and freedom.

A caveat: I'm always somewhat skeptical about brief personality quizzes because humans are complex, diverse and multi-faceted and don't easily fit into neat boxes. These theories can never claim universality. I took the Four Tendencies quiz and found that Rubin's framework gave me some insight and clarity.

I'll share my quiz results and an example of how I use the information to think about a self-care goal:

My dominant tendency is Upholder. I've been trying to do a daily morning walk because morning light has been shown to improve nighttime sleep quality.

- As an Upholder, I can mostly motivate myself to do it. At first, I relied on tracking my steps, but this can't be my main strategy because too much tracking can trigger the old, rigid diet culture mentality in me (more on this in Weeks 22 and 35).

- It helps me to have some external validation and community care. So, I have been talking to friends about this goal as a way to stay accountable. I sometimes enjoy a walking buddy but not every day. Every so often, I help a friend by borrowing their dog.

- Thinking ahead, I might need extra motivational support for this habit when winter comes. I resonated a bit with the Questioner tendency, so it might help me to research the benefits of cold-weather walks.

If I found that I had another dominant tendency, my approach might be different:

- **Obligers:** I could find external accountability and community through a walking group.

- **Questioners:** I could research the best ways to stay motivated with walking.

- **Rebels:** I could figure out my best process by noticing my own motivation. No one else's strategies or expectations matter.

Here's this week's experiment:

- If you're curious, take the five-minute Four Tendencies quiz on Gretchen Rubin's website (see www.farzanadoctor.com/52weeks for a link).

_____

_____

_____

_____

- After checking out the tendencies, think about how you've been doing with moving through this book or with a specific self-care goal. Did the Four Tendencies framework help you to understand your process?

_____

_____

_____

_____

TIPS Like all theories and frameworks about human behaviour, remember that this won't work for everyone. Use these ideas for expanding self-understanding, but don't pigeonhole yourself. If it pleases you to use a label from this framework, go for it. Otherwise, add the new information to your toolbox in a more general way.

WEEK 22
Habit Stacking

IN WEEK 14, I suggested stacking the practice of noticing your nervous system's state of arousal onto another established habit, such as eating lunch, brushing your teeth or turning on your computer. This concept is called *habit stacking*.

The term was first coined by S.J. Scott in his 2014 book *Habit Stacking: 97 Small Life Changes That Take Five Minutes or Less*. However, I first learned the strategy in the late nineties when I was trying (and failing) to remember to take a nutritional supplement. A friend suggested that I put the supplement on my kitchen table so that I'd remember to take it with breakfast.

Eventually breakfast, a regular morning habit, became the automatic cue for taking the supplement. Years later, I no longer need to leave the supplement on the table.

Other examples:

A meditation leader once explained to our class that he wakes up, uses the toilet and immediately sits on his cushion. In other words, he's stacked meditation onto his morning pee! This sets up a chain of behaviours that helps him start the day well (see more on this in Week 25).

I type case notes and send out invoices after each client session. This stacking helps me to not avoid these tedious administrative tasks. To facilitate this, I give myself a thirty-minute window (see Week 10) between sessions so I have enough time. In the leftover fifteen minutes of break time, I stretch, go to the bathroom, drink water, daydream, reflect on vicarious trauma (see Week 27), grab a snack or dance out tension.

Here's an example of habit stacking with a habit I'd like to shift:

Like many people, I crave sugar after meals. For the last few years, I've turned this into an auto-cue by eating refined sugar after every meal (an example of how neuroplasticity—Week 5—works). While I love dessert, I'd like to not make this a three-times-a-day habit. Instead, I'd like to eat more fruit. To address this:

- I can stack fruit onto my meals by ensuring the fruit bowl is in the middle of my kitchen table and full of stuff I love. Of course, I can eat a refined sugar dessert if I really want it. Note that this is an additive, gentle nutrition approach rather than a deprivation and diet approach (more on this distinction in this week's Deeper Dive).

- I will repeat this practice daily for a month so that my auto-cue is for fruit, rather than refined sugar, after a meal.

Wish me luck!

Here's this week's experiment:

- Think back over the last months. Choose one self-care practice you've valued but haven't yet made into a well-established habit. How might you stack it onto an established habit? Or choose a negative habit you'd like to break. What new habit could you stack on to interrupt it?

Deeper Dive

Gentle nutrition is a principle that comes from the intuitive eating framework created by Evelyn Tribole and Elyse Resch in their 2012 book *Intuitive Eating: A Revolutionary Anti-Diet Approach*.

I include this information here because for many, food and eating are part of self-care journeys. It's also a common way that we care for others (with meal trains for sick friends, for example, or cakes for co-workers' birthdays, or simply cooking for our families). But food and eating are fraught for many because we live in a fat-phobic culture in which so many of us grow up feeling shame and hatred towards our bodies.

Gentle nutrition is an anti-diet approach that encourages adding in foods that you enjoy and that support your health. There are no "good" or "bad" foods, just food. For those of us recovering from the trauma of diet culture, this approach can be healing.

Additive approaches work better than deprivation strategies for many self-care goals. Deprivation sets us up to over-focus on what we "can't have" while additive approaches help us to focus on what we need and desire.

If these ideas resonate for you, check out *Intuitive Eating*, and also look for *The Body Is Not an Apology: The Power of Radical Self-Love* by Sonya Renee Taylor.

WEEK 23

Conscious
Intention-Setting

CONSCIOUS INTENTION-SETTING can be a gentle but powerful way to stay connected to your desires and goals.

Here are the steps for setting an intention:

1 Go inward. You can do this through formal meditation, or simply by pausing and breathing and asking yourself what you want to accomplish. I often set an intention for "energy, calm and insight as I do my work." That's fairly general. You could be more specific: "I intend to be kind to myself while I try this new skill" or "I intend to take my breaks today."

2 Once you've brought the intention to consciousness, mentally repeat it three times or write it down. The repetition helps to focus the mind.

3 If you have a spiritual practice, ask for assistance with the intention. If you don't, skip this step.

4 If you are someone who does better with external accountability and support (see Week 21), share your intention with a loved one, and if it makes sense, ask for assistance or reminders. You could also share it on social media to access community care.

5 Later, check in with yourself. How did you do? If there were obstacles, set your next intention to cover how you'd like to handle them.

This can be done with teams, groups or pairs. For example, I've often asked the couples I work with to set an intention for the week, based on whatever we've been addressing in session. There is a palpable energy shift when people co-create an intention.

Here's this week's experiment:

* What intention would you like to set today for your self-care or community care goals? Try the steps outlined above and see how it goes this week.

_____

_____

_____

_____

_____

TIPS For most of us, it's a good idea to detach from the outcome of the intention because this puts too much pressure on yourself and your goal. Instead of looking at this as a pass-or-fail exercise, consider a process-oriented approach. Notice reactions and learning, be curious about obstacles and acknowledge and validate your feelings, rather than focussing on the outcome of your intention-setting.

WEEK 24

Review and Reflection

PAT YOURSELF on the back! You're almost halfway through this journey! In addition to reviewing the past three weeks, you might find it interesting to do another quarterly review of the Self- and Community Care Wheel (Week 3). Have you noticed any shifts?

This month addressed motivation and habits and how to use this information to help with self-care and community care goals.

Take a few minutes to revisit and absorb this month's content, and to complete or repeat experiments that interested you. Here's a checklist of what we explored in the experiments:

Learn about Your Motivation Tendency

☐ Complete the Four Tendencies quiz. Does the framework help you to better understand your approach to reaching self-care or community care goals?

Habit Stacking

☐ Try out habit stacking to strengthen a new habit or weaken another.

Conscious Intention-Setting

☐ Use intention-setting to assist you with a self-care or community care goal.

MONTH
SEVEN

Over the next month, we'll
focus on awareness of mood.

WEEK 25

Are Your Mornings a Drag?

MORNINGS CAN be hard for many of us. This may be the result of programming that was neuroplastically (yup, Week 5 again) created.

My memories of mornings: my (probably sleep-deprived and overwhelmed) mother's instructions to not speak to her before her first cup of tea, being super hangry (I was hypoglycemic as a kid) and the stress of rushing to school. I don't recall calm in the morning.

I carried this unconscious learning into my adult life, deciding that, just like my mom, I wasn't a "morning person."

How we begin our day can set the tone for the day's self- and community care.

If you did learn to have crappy mornings, the good news is that it's possible to reprogram yourself. I learned this by accident.

Sixteen years ago, I adopted a one-year-old rescue dog named Maggie. Each morning, she showed up at my bedside, tail wagging, expectant and happy. I'd groan and say sarcastically (because, clearly, her morning happiness was inappropriate): "It's a brand new day!"

Over time (because dogs don't care that you're not a morning person and they absolutely don't care about your sarcasm) Maggie wore me down. Each morning, she arrived by my bedside, happy, and I began to notice that I was saying "It's a brand new day!" with a laugh, then with gratitude. I actually started to *believe* it was a brand new day and feel grateful about it.

My dog reprogrammed me. Dogs are so smart.

That little bit of gratitude begot more. Now, I say thank you for everything I can think of when I first wake up.

Thank you for this brand new day!
Thank you for this glass of water on my bedside table! I was thirsty!
Thank you for electricity! For the sun shining!
And so on.

There is a growing field of research on the science of gratitude and positive psychology.

One widely quoted study is by psychologists Robert Emmons and Michael McCullough. In 2003, they examined the effect of a grateful outlook on psychological and physical well-being. They assigned subjects into three groups, and each recorded either their week's hassles, or things they were grateful for, or neutral life events. After ten weeks, the gratitude group was more optimistic, exercised more and had fewer doctor's visits.

It's also worth noting that as humans, we have a negativity bias—a tendency to pay attention to and learn from negative information—which has helped us survive as a species. Awareness of this can help us to lean in the opposite direction.

But what about *toxic positivity*?

Positive psychology has been criticized for ignoring context and emphasizing positive affect over negative experience. I think it's about balance; it's important to not bypass our uncomfortable feelings and truths. Gratitude practice needs to incorporate understandings of oppression and emotional and physical pain.

I like morning gratitude as a way to begin the day if I'm starting with a blank slate. However, if I wake up in pain, or with big feelings from a nightmare, I'll start with acknowledging those before moving on to gratitude.

Rose, Bud, Thorn

One activity I like for balance is Rose, Bud, Thorn, where we list one thing from each category (in whatever order you like).

- Thorn (a hard thing):
  - My neck hurts.

- Bud (something in development):
  - I'm meeting a friend later today and I'm looking forward to that.

- Rose (something we are grateful for or feeling joy about):
  - I'm grateful I got some rest.

Here's this week's experiment:

- What did you learn about mornings from your childhood? How are mornings for you now?

_____

_____

_____

_____

_____

- Name three things you're grateful for upon waking. Try it for a week. How do you feel? If you're not feeling good upon waking, don't bypass the harder feelings. Try Rose, Bud, Thorn instead.

_____

_____

_____

_____

_____

TIPS Note that it's possible to find gratitude in ordinary things (a soft pillow, a cup of coffee, running water), which is important because few of us wake up to breakfast in bed, rainbows and glitter.

If you feel groggy upon waking and find it hard to remember this experiment, leave a note with a list of gratitude statements beside your bed. Or adopt a dog.

WEEK 26

Low Moods and
Their Triggers

THIS WEEK, we look at ways we can understand mood, identify low-mood triggers and sort out needs. We'll also look at quick relief hacks.

But first some background on mood.

Our thoughts can trigger our emotions, which affect our mood.

Low moods are part of being human. Sometimes the low-mood trigger is identifiable, and sometimes it's difficult to identify.

A caveat: if your low moods are consistently a hardship for you, or debilitating, seek professional help to address their deeper emotional and physical causes.

Low mood and work

Those of us who work with people or causes might notice that our low moods can be triggered by the work. For example, while there is much satisfaction, meaning and joy in my work as a social worker, I know I'm more exposed to the sadder and more painful side of life than most. The same goes for my gender justice activism.

It's useful to understand low-mood triggers so that we can address them. If a sudden low mood hits you, ask yourself:

- What happened in the last hour or day that might have upset me?

- Who did I talk to? What did I just read, listen to or watch?

- What's happening in my body right now?

- What meaning am I making about this? What are my thoughts, beliefs, perceptions about it?

- What might I need? Would support from others help right now? Would a limit or boundary make sense?

Here are a few examples of my own low-mood triggers and how I address them:

Trigger: This evening I spent too much time on social media, which has led to self-deprecating thoughts (aah, negative comparisons to other people!) and this has left me feeling low.

Need: a time limit for how long I spend on social media. Or perhaps I can use a social media–based mood elevator (see below).

Trigger: I've been busier in my activism. There have been more meetings and I think it's leading to me having anxious thoughts and feelings of apathy.

Need: a short break from this work, or to pace it differently. I might need to talk to my activist buddies about this. Maybe they are feeling the same way and we can support each other.

Trigger: I've been working with a client who is coping with particularly disturbing memories of violence. I find myself feeling more rage than is probably healthy for me (to clarify, some rage is useful and helps me get stuff done!). I may be holding some of the emotional residue from exposure to her trauma stories.

Need: Acknowledging the vicarious trauma helps me to let it go (see more on this in Week 27). If the feelings persist, I'll need to get some support from my peer supervision group.

Sometimes we need quicker relief when we feel stuck in a difficult mood. *Mood elevators* can be useful hacks in these moments and might steady us enough to allow for deeper reflection. Here are some of mine:

- Social media posts. #AnimalFriendship makes me laugh. #SomaticHealing reels remind me to complete the stress response cycle (see Week 13).

- Music can stop negative thinking. I have a couple of playlists dedicated to this. I get bonus mood benefits if I force myself to dance to them and down-regulate. (See Week 15 for more on somatic hacks.)

- Napping or just lying down.

- Guided mindfulness meditations help me to shake off my thoughts and "wake up" to the moment.

- Intentionally relaxing the face and smiling (even a forced smile) has been shown to help us release serotonin (which reduces feelings of stress) and dopamine (which increases feelings of happiness). Yes, smiling works as a mood hack.

- Holding self-compassion for my low mood. Researcher Kristin Neff has written about how self-compassion can decrease cortisol levels. I like to imagine bathing myself in self-compassion. This will reduce any feelings of self-judgment I might be holding and allow me to be with my feelings more comfortably.

Triggers and community care

Understanding triggers is essential for self-care and has benefits for those around us. If we're mindful of triggers, we can slow down, reduce reactivity and avoid being unfairly critical or defensive. When we are triggered, we can create unnecessary tension or urgency in our projects and reinforce a culture of overwork.

If you notice your loved ones, co-workers or activist buddies having a hard time, you might gently guide them to look at triggers and needs.

Here's this week's experiment:

- Make your own list of triggers as you encounter them this week. Beside your list of triggers, brainstorm the needs, limits or boundaries that might help.

_____

_____

_____

_____

_____

_____

_____

_____

- How often does a low mood get triggered by your helping or activist work? We'll address this more next week.

_____

_____

_____

_____

- Make your own list of mood elevators for quick relief.

_____

_____

_____

_____

TIPS

- If you're having trouble identifying the trigger for a persistent low mood, use the HALT strategy from Alcoholics Anonymous. HALT stands for Hungry? Angry? Lonely? Tired? Ask yourself these questions as a *starting point* for your self-reflection. If you find you are angry or lonely, those feelings can reveal others. At least half the time when I'm feeling low it's because I'm hungry or tired, or because of other body-based discomforts that can be tended to in some way.

- Consider combining these ideas with your list of somatic resources from Week 14 if your low mood comes from being in hyper- or hypo-arousal.

WEEK 27

Letting Go of
Sticky Feelings

WHEN WE work with people, we can absorb their feelings, even if we are using strategies to prevent this from happening (for example, the energy techniques in Week 19). We need to identify this, understand which feelings are ours (and which do not belong to us) and attend to them. Doing this can help prevent or address vicarious traumatization and burnout (Week 11).

Here's my sticky feelings technique:

1 Take a moment to breathe and ground (see the sidebar at the end of the chapter for grounding strategies).

2 List the interactions you've had that day or week in your care or activist work. Or, if you deal with a lot of people, list the people or interactions that were *particularly memorable*. Beside each, write a word or two about the content of the interaction and any sticky feelings (those that are still with you after the interaction).

Mine might look like this:

NAME	CONTENT	STICKY FEELING
BZ (client)	Racism at work	Frustration and anger
LL (client)	Anxiety	Worry
JY (client)	Boundaries	None
Marika (friend)	Relationship stuff	Anger at her partner
Fatima (activist buddy)	Lack of momentum with a campaign	Hopelessness and apathy
Pekoe (dog)	Has been at the shelter for over 100 days	Heartbreak

- Acknowledge the feelings with compassion. Take a breath and release them, reminding yourself that the feelings were absorbed and might not belong to you. Likely, this will be enough to release them. This worked well with the conversation with LL.

- If the feelings are still sticky: 1) be clear about your role or responsibility and 2) the other's abilities and resources, and 3) notice any personal triggers or countertransference. For example:

BZ:

1   My role was to help her process her feelings.

2   She's more than capable of working through her next steps.

3   But! The conversation brought up some old memories about a similar experience I had with a boss, and I'll need to take a minute to acknowledge them and maybe talk to a friend or therapist about them.

Marika:

1   My role as a friend is to hold space. I don't have to fix anything or protect her from her partner's disrespect.

2   She's insightful and has a community that can support her.

3   No personal triggers.

Fatima:

1   My role is as an activist buddy and I can hold space if I have capacity.

2   She's new to this activism, and easily triggered, and I'm just one of her supports.

3   I have my own difficult feelings about the campaign and the larger systemic issues that block progress. I can share these with Fatima and ask if she can support me too.

Pekoe:

1   My role was to do my best during my three-hour volunteer shift.

2   I am part of a much larger team and system that cares for these animals.

3   Some of my own grief about my dog's death is saying hello. I'll need to sit with that.

Yes, boundaries again!

Reminding ourselves of our role or responsibility in care and activist work is about reminding ourselves of our boundaries in the work. If you have trouble with this, review Weeks 17–19.

Here's this week's experiment:

• Notice how often you take on, or get triggered by, others' feelings in your care or activist work. Do you go to bed thinking about them or perseverate during time off? Do you sometimes feel emotionally low or depleted at the end of the day and not know why?

_____

_____

_____

_____

- Try the sticky feelings technique at least twice this week. Perhaps do it as a pairs exercise with a co-worker or friend. Make notes here or keep a separate "sticky feelings" journal if you'd like to notice ongoing trends and patterns.

_____

_____

_____

_____

_____

Getting grounded

There are thousands of *grounding strategies*. Here are some of my favourite quick ones:

- Plant your feet. Notice the sensations of your toes, balls of feet and heels as they touch the ground.

- Inhale for a count of three, then exhale for a count of six. Repeat three times.

- Come to your senses. Notice one thing you hear, see, taste, smell and touch.

- Do a quick body scan, from head to toe, noticing and accepting (or being kind to) all sensations.

- Visualize your spine as a tree trunk with roots reaching down through your feet and branches and leaves through your arms.

- Go outside. If you can, walk barefoot. Touch tree trunks. Notice insects, birds, animals and flowers.

- Connect to the back of your body: become aware of your spine, lengthen it, and feel the energy running from your tailbone up to your head.

- Use water. Drink it, splash it on your face or slowly wash your hands.

WEEK 28
Review and Reflection

THESE LAST three weeks were all about noticing mood, triggers and dealing with emotional residue from care or activist work.

Take a few minutes to revisit and absorb this month's content, and to complete or repeat experiments that interested you. Here's a checklist of what we explored in the experiments:

Are Your Mornings a Drag?

☐ Consider what you learned about mornings in childhood.

☐ Try the gratitude practice or the Rose, Bud, Thorn exercise upon waking.

Low Moods and Their Triggers

☐ Make a list of triggers as you encounter them over a week.

☐ Identify how often a low mood gets triggered by your helping or activist work.

☐ Make a list of quick-relief mood elevators.

Letting Go of Sticky Feelings

☐ Notice how often you take on, or get triggered by, others' feelings in your care or activist work.

☐ Try the sticky feelings technique, perhaps as a pairs exercise with a co-worker or friend.

A REMINDER Use these review weeks to look over the material from the previous weeks, reflect on what worked and remain curious about this process. You can also use this week to catch up on or repeat activities that were especially interesting to you.

MONTH
EIGHT

This month, we'll look at attachment
and asking for help as important aspects
of self- and community care.

WEEK 29

Attachment

ATTACHMENT THEORY changed my life. It taught me how and why I was having trouble feeling safe in relationships, and how to allow myself to give and take love and care more easily. It helped me to more compassionately understand my reactions to triggers and conflict.

As you read this section, reflect on your relationships with co-workers, loved ones, clients or patients and activist buddies.

> According to psychologist John Bowlby, how we experienced attachment from our primary caregivers during our first two years will usually predict our *attachment style* in our adult lives.

How well supported our caregivers were (their access to health and emotional care, affordable childcare, helpful community, rest, financial security, etc.) will have an impact on how well they were able to attune and attach to their babies. In other words, attachment is structural.

Attachment styles represent a set of tendencies we have when in close relationships, and are especially noticeable when we feel stressed, insecure or threatened.

The four attachment style categories are:

1 Anxious (also referred to as Preoccupied)

2 Avoidant (also referred to as Dismissive)

3 Disorganized (also referred to as Fearful-Avoidant)

4 Secure

For a full explanation of these styles, see the Deeper Dive.

Attachment theory tends to focus on connection with romantic partners, but we can extend attachment beyond this—for example, to extended and chosen family, animals, plants, our homes, our cultures, ancestors, the earth and more. All of this can influence our sense of belonging and safety in the world.

This theory also tends to focus on how we were parented or treated by caregivers, but experiences (both traumatic and nurturing) with other family members, or people at school or other communities, can potentially reinforce or repair early attachment injuries.

As adults, with awareness and healing, we can learn to be more secure-functioning in our relationships.

It's useful to map our tendencies so that we can normalize and communicate our needs and find ways to calm ourselves in times of relational conflict. When we know our own operating manual, we can share it with loved ones. It's also good to know our loved ones' operating manuals so that we can avoid inadvertently and unnecessarily distressing them.

Knowing about attachment and working toward being more secure-functioning in our relationships can help us to understand how we operate with individuals and groups in our helping or activist work. It might allow us to sort out what makes us *reactive* to the people we work with. It can also help us give and receive care.

Here's this week's experiment:

- This week, take a few minutes to reflect on your relationships with co-workers, loved ones, clients or patients, activist friends and the larger community. Are there places of ease? Places of discomfort? How might attachment intersect with this?

_____

_____

_____

_____

_____

- If you're new to this, see www.farzanadoctor.com/52weeks for a three-minute attachment styles quiz.

TIPS

- Avoid using attachment styles as labels, unless that pleases you. I've intentionally used the term "tendencies" because it's important we don't pathologize ourselves or others. Most people will resonate with one dominant style or tendency, but others may not. For example, they might notice that in one relationship they were more anxious, while in another, they felt more avoidant.

- You might be wondering what secure-functioning means. This will vary from person to person, but generally, a secure-functioning relationship or group will value and enact mutuality, respect, fairness, attunement and affection. It will feel safe and secure. When there is harm or conflict, there is quick repair.

Deeper Dive

This is a complex topic that is difficult to briefly summarize without being over-simplistic. Go to www.farzanadoctor.com/52weeks, where you'll find a link to an article by psychologist Diane Poole Heller that describes the four attachment styles, and common ways they are expressed in adult relationships.

You may also want to read *Wired for Love* by Stan Tatkin, or *Polysecure: Attachment, Trauma and Consensual Nonmonogamy* by Jessica Fern.

WEEK 30
Asking for Help

WE ARE social beings who are interdependent on others. We need to give and receive help both during ordinary times and during crises. This week's focus will be on the more ordinary times, and next week we'll look at crises.

Think about a (non-crisis) time when you needed help. Were you able to ask? To what extent were you able to be vulnerable? What made it easy or hard for you?

Here are some non-crisis examples from my own life:

- Asking a friend or partner to accompany me to a medical appointment

- Getting some reassurance from my stepmother on a housing decision

- Asking a friend to hold space about an interpersonal conflict

- Asking a colleague to listen to worries about work

- Using writing sprints to feel accompanied when writing is not easy (this is a form of "body doubling." See this week's Deeper Dive to learn more about how this works.)

- Asking people to be beta readers for this book

It isn't always comfortable for me to ask for help.

Maybe you're the same. Do you intellectually understand that being vulnerable and relying on others is a necessary part of (and beneficial to) friendship, collegiality or community, but have trouble doing so? If so, you're not alone. Most of the helpers and activists I know have trouble asking for help.

Why it's hard to ask for help

Here are just some of the reasons people struggle so much to ask for help:

- We worry about being a burden on others (they're busy and have their own problems).

- It feels uncomfortable, scary or like too much work.

- If we do ask, the help might not be "right" and then we'll just have to "fix" things ourselves anyway.

- In the past when we asked for help, we ended up having to emotionally take care of the person who was supposed to be listening to or helping us.

- We sometimes make the motions of receiving support, but don't lean into it deeply or immediately feel the need to reciprocate in order to not "owe" anyone. Receiving help leaves us feeling guilt.

- We seek support only after we've sorted things out, so what we share is more like a report or summary. Perhaps we share more about our resilience rather than our vulnerabilities.

- Internalized capitalism and ableism might have enforced the idea that we're supposed to handle everything on our own.

- Our early life and its traumas might have taught us that asking for help is a dangerous exercise. For example, maybe:

  - Help was not readily available when we needed it.

  - When we did ask for help we were not believed or were turned away.

  - Receiving help came with judgment, ridicule, criticism or other negative consequences.

  - Offers of help came with "strings attached" (we were expected to reciprocate in ways that weren't fair).

  - Other experiences or messages taught us it was better to be self-reliant rather than to ask for or accept help.

Last week's glance at attachment might give you further insight into what makes it difficult or easy to ask for and receive support. For example: it took me a long time to feel safe asking for help because I learned to adapt to insecure attachment (and the disappointment of inconsistent attunement) by being the "good" (not needy) kid in the family.

If you relate to pieces of this, remember that it's possible to shift beliefs and behaviours.

And if you'd like more self-care and community care in your life, it will be essential to balance out the care you give with the care you ask for and receive.

Here's this week's experiment:

- Jot down your reactions to the list of reasons why people struggle to ask for help. What struck a chord? What might you add to the list?

_____

_____

_____

_____

- Look back at last week's recap on attachment. How might your tendencies around attachment connect to your ability to ask for help?

_____

_____

_____

_____

_____

· Think back to a recent time in your life when you tried to ask for help. In hindsight, could you have leaned in a bit more? Were there any expressions of support or care that you might have consciously or unconsciously turned away?

_____

_____

_____

_____

_____

· Reach out for support once this week. Notice any resistance or hesitation. Was there a homeostatic impulse (Week 6)?

_____

_____

_____

_____

_____

TIP Speak to a trusted person (perhaps someone who's known you for a long time) or a professional who can give you feedback and support about your tendencies around asking for help.

Deeper Dive

Body doubling is a strategy, coined by coach and mentor Linda Anderson in 1996, that has since become popular among ADHD (attention deficit hyperactivity disorder) and other communities of neurodiverse people. A body double is someone who works alongside you, either in the same room or virtually, on a similar or different task. Being in the presence of others can be calming and motivating and help you start and complete projects that might be intimidating, tedious or otherwise challenging to do alone.

Examples:

- A three-hour Zoom meeting where strangers and friends gather to clear their email inboxes

- Two friends hanging out while organizing their taxes

- Virtual writing sprint groups or writing meetups in coffee shops

- Facetiming a loved one while you both clean your homes or do laundry

WEEK 31

Support during
Hard Times

LAST WEEK we looked at why many people have trouble asking for help. This can be even harder during the hard times, when the stakes feel higher. Here's a common example:

> A nurse I know is experiencing burnout. Over the last few tiring years, she stopped many of her leisure and social activities and now feels isolated. She's sad most of the time. I ask her, "Who can you call on in a crisis like this?" She tells me she doesn't like to burden others with her troubles. And when she does talk to her loved ones, they get so dysregulated that she ends up having to take care of them.

I've learned that support works best when people know *how* to help us in these hard moments, and vice versa. Here are a few examples of how that knowledge can help:

- I have a friend who rarely reaches out, and so when she texts me "do you have some time to talk today?" I know that this is her version of an SOS. In fact, we've talked about this. I call her as soon as I am able.

- When I was going through a break-up, a friend sent me daily texts asking, "How is today, friend?" I'd reply with something like, "It's a seesaw of emotions. Thanks for checking in." She would reply with, "Need anything?" and I'd say, "No, but your check-in really helps." That became our system for a while. (In hindsight, I could have leaned in more to her offers. It took me a while to learn that I wasn't doing this enough with my friends.)

- Another friend went through a health crisis and asked for visits and meal deliveries. A community of friends set up a shared calendar so that we could schedule ourselves most efficiently. We understood exactly what kind of help was wanted and needed.

With these three examples, it's important to note that these relationships are mutual and reciprocal. This is the way I prefer things to be, but in some situations, the care and help might be one-way and that might be appropriate— for example, when assistance is coming from professionals, or from an adult to a child. Or sometimes care between two adults is reciprocal for a period of time and at another time non-reciprocal. My partner's care of his mother, who is in the last stage of Alzheimer's, is an example of this.

If receiving support isn't going smoothly, examine whether you have given specific enough instructions on how you need to be supported in both crisis and non-crisis times. This sets up a positive experience for both parties. For example:

One of my clients wants to reach out to her father in a crisis, but she knows that talking about feelings isn't his strength, and the conversation will make him anxious. He will problem-solve in a way that she doesn't find helpful. This in turn will leave my client feeling unheard and unsupported and she might get angry at him. She'll end up not calling and he'll want to avoid her calls!

HER SOLUTION: She asked him to check in during crises and to only offer distraction and social engagement, which helps her calm. Talking about her father's book club and gossiping about the neighbours worked for them both. The instructions meant my client got her needs met, and her dad knew exactly what to do.

What do *you* usually need when you're having a hard moment? Problem-solving? Listening? Feedback? Help with tasks? Perhaps you want different things at different times and from different people?

On the other hand, if you're the person being called on for support, how might you ask your loved one what they need so that you're in sync?

If you're still having trouble receiving support, another area to examine is the people in your circle. A trend I've seen among those who find it hard to ask for help is that they may have accumulated friends who aren't particularly emotionally sensitive or giving. Old patterns of being the giver in relationships, and perhaps attracting people who are "familiar" (meaning they replicate the patterns in one's family of origin) take time to change.

The nurse I referenced at the beginning of this chapter gave some thought to how to reach out to two friends. She let them know that she was burnt out and needed them to hold space for her so that she could sort out her next steps. She made it clear that she only wanted them to listen so she would feel less alone. She told them that problem-solving would only add to her overwhelm. After some time, she felt better and asked one for help to strategize how to take a leave of absence from her work.

Here's this week's experiment:

Make a list of three people you'd like to have in your personal support network. If you can't think of at least three, talk to a friend or counsellor about how to build your network. You may have to work through some of the feelings from Week 30 in order to create this list.

- Beside each name, list the kinds of support you might want to ask for in a crisis. Pitch to their strengths.

- Reach out and let them know about this exercise and talk about mutual needs. Or, the next time you're having a hard time, reach out to them and ask them if they can offer the kind of support you need ("Hi, I'm having a hard time right now. Do you have bandwidth to listen to me today?" or "I'm feeling really anxious today. Do you have time and energy to come over and watch TV with me?").

- If your support person veers off course (for example, advice-giving when you've only asked for listening), gently interrupt them and remind them of what support would be better for you.

NAME   **SUPPORT TO ASK FOR**

_____   _____

_____   _____

_____   _____

Holding space

Holding space is an important skill to learn. To do it:

- Remain present and grounded (see Week 27).

- Listen *without* problem-solving.

- Ask deepening questions to help the speaker express themselves further. A simple "tell me more about that" suffices if you're not sure what to ask.

- You might offer an empathetic statement like, "I'm so sorry you're going through this." You can also ask, "Is there anything else you need?"

- Remember that you don't have to fix anything.

- Pay attention to your own boundaries (Weeks 17 and 18), including your energetic boundaries (Week 19). Stick with what your time and energy allow.

Review and Reflection

IT'S BEEN eight months already! Well done.

This last month has focussed on attachment, our relationships and asking for and receiving care.

Take a few minutes to revisit and absorb this month's content, and to complete or repeat experiments that interested you. Here's a checklist of what we explored in the experiments:

Attachment

☐ Reflect on your relationships.

☐ Take the three-minute attachment styles quiz to better understand your attachment style and tendencies.

Asking for Help

☐ Notice your reactions to the list of reasons why people struggle to ask for help.

☐ Consider how attachment might connect to your ability to ask for help.

☐ Reach out for support and notice your feelings.

Support during Hard Times

☐ List three people you'd like to have in your personal support network and identify the kinds of support you might want to ask for in a crisis.

☐ Reach out and discuss this exercise with them. Talk about mutual needs in times of crisis.

MONTH
NINE

This month, we return to the body,
and ways we can use awareness to
strengthen self- and community care.

If you'd like, review some of
the concepts from Weeks 13–15.

WEEK 33
PEACE Breathing

SOMETIMES, AT the end of a workday, I can feel spaced out or numb. If I've been in autopilot mode all day, I might not notice that something has triggered a mood shift (see Week 26) or there is overwhelm in my nervous system, taking me into hypo-arousal (Week 14).

Here's a quick activity that helps me to emotionally and physically shift. I learned and adapted it from Guiomar Campbell, my shiatsu and acupuncture therapist for many years. It's a favourite of mine because it includes mindfulness and self-compassion concepts, and its acronym makes it easy to use.

This is also a good activity for tuning in to sticky feelings or vicarious trauma (Week 27). Try this right now as you read.

P: Pause for 5 seconds. Stop what you're doing and tune in to your mind and body.

E: Exhale. Now breathe, allowing your exhalations to be twice as long as your inhalations (i.e., breathe in for 3 counts, breathe out for 6 counts, and repeat this 3 times).

Total time: 27 seconds.

A: Acknowledge any feelings or sensations in the body. Greet them nonjudgmentally. For example: "Hello, sadness" or "Hello, tightness in my shoulders." Don't go into any stories or evaluations or analysis or problem-solving! Just acknowledge feelings and sensations.

Total time: 20 seconds.

C: Be **compassionate** to yourself the way a best friend might respond to you and your struggles. Or if it's easier, imagine what you'd say to your best friend. You might say, "Oh, honey, I'm sorry you're feeling sad." Or you might visualize sending love from your heart to whatever part of your body needs it.

Another way to feel compassion is to remember that a million people might be feeling this exact emotion or sensation right now too. You're not alone. You're human. Why not send compassion to the other million too?

Self-compassion calms the amygdala. Notice if you feel calmer.

Total time: 20 seconds.

E: Repeat the first E. Breathe, allowing your **exhalations** to be twice as long as your inhalations (i.e., breathe in for 3 counts, breathe out for 6 counts, and repeat 3 times).

Total time: 27 seconds.

Here's this week's experiment:

• Try the PEACE breathing technique once a day. Use habit stacking (Week 22) or a sticky note as a reminder.

> **TIPS** Let's tie a few concepts together. Longer exhalations activate the parasympathetic nervous system—also known as the "rest and digest" branch of the nervous system—and signal safety, which can help us to complete the stress response cycle (Week 13) and return to the Window of Capacity (Week 14).

Deeper Dive

• Research has shown that mindfulness-based stress reduction (MBSR) can literally change our brains. MBSR is associated with changes in grey matter concentration in regions involved in emotional regulation, empathy, perspective taking, learning and memory. See www.farzanadoctor.com/52weeks to watch an eight-minute TEDx talk by neuroscientist Sara Lazar.

• If you're new to mindfulness, or could use a refresher, consider taking a course. See www.farzanadoctor.com/52weeks for a link to a free mindfulness course offered by Tara Brach and Jack Kornfield. Each lesson is ten to fifteen minutes in length and has a combination of information and meditation practice. It's a good one to do with a buddy or a group.

WEEK 34

Is Your Body Saying No?

OUR BODIES and minds are connected. The more we tune in and acknowledge our body's sensations, the more literate and fluent we become in understanding our emotions and our emotional needs.

Here are some examples of the mind-body connection, where emotions are experienced in physical sensations: grief can feel like heaviness around the heart, nervous anticipation as "butterflies" in the belly, fear as the hair on the back of the neck standing up, anxiety as constriction in the throat or burning in the pit of the stomach.

According to Gabor Maté, a Canadian physician, writer and speaker, when we suppress our emotional distress, the body can react by saying no through illness, pain and disease, and caregivers and helping professionals need to be especially aware of this. A tendency to be over-focussed on duty, obligation and caring for others before ourselves are risk factors for poor health.

This makes sense, right? When we pull focus from our well-being, while consistently absorbing others' pain, we are less able to notice the subtle and obvious physical cues that tell us we need rest and care. Or if we do notice, we might have learned to push through or ignore them because others' needs feel more pressing. To be clear, this is not your fault! As I described in the introduction to this book, this tendency may be an adaptation to adverse childhood experiences.

An antidote to this is mindful awareness. Tune in to your body right now, scanning from head to toe. Notice (non-judgmentally) the sensations in your body:

- Where is there ease, pleasure, pain or tension?
- What do these sensations tell you about your feelings?
- Are you trying to push past or ignore these sensations?
- What do you need?

When I tuned in, I received this feedback:

- My tight shoulders tell me I'm feeling anxious about a deadline. I might need to talk through the worry with someone or write about it or stretch to loosen up.

- A flare-up of a patch of eczema on my back is a reminder that my stress levels are too high.

- I may need to move the deadline, or if I can't do that, I may have to lighten up on other tasks to give myself a break.

Here's this week's experiment:

- Do the body scan daily.

- If your body is saying no, can you listen to it? Note that rest doesn't have to look like a radical change (although it might). You can find shorter rests through naps, guided meditations, daydreaming, a slow walk or better sleep at night (see Week 42).

_____

_____

_____

_____

- Also notice when your body says yes. What situations or activities give you ease, pleasure and joy?

_____

_____

_____

_____

_____

Deeper Dive

If you'd like to learn more about Gabor Maté's work, check out *When the Body Says No: The Cost of Hidden Stress* or *The Myth of Normal: Trauma, Illness and Healing in a Toxic Culture.* He's a prolific speaker and many of his talks are available online.

WEEK 35

A Body-Neutral
Approach to Movement

IN WEEK 13, we talked about physical activity as one of the tools for completing the stress response cycle.

But this can be complicated—societal fat phobia and ableism can leave many of us with negative relationships to exercise, "fitness," movement and body image. I know it's complicated for me.

My mother, who was slim her whole life, seemed to always be on a diet. As a kid, I tagged along to her Weight Watchers meetings, witnessing stressful weigh-ins and body shaming. My father was an avid exerciser and marathoner. I picked up positive and negative beliefs and habits about food and exercise from them both. And of course, my community and the media reinforced body and appearance myths too.

For many years I was consumed by diet culture, and exercise often felt like punishment or compensation for eating too much. Every lap I ran or swam was about burning calories and trying to change my brown, femme, round body into something that resembled the fat-phobic, white-supremacist, ableist and misogynistic beauty industry standard.

It has taken years to unlearn this, and I'm still unlearning. Every so often, when I am not consciously resisting fat-phobic messages, one of them will sneak in and trigger me. I need regular reminders! This is especially true these days as I notice my perimenopausal body changing (as it's supposed to). I intentionally seek out articles, videos and fitness instructors who have body-neutral approaches to movement to continue the process of liberating myself.

What is body neutrality?

- **Appreciating function:** Using movement and activity to improve or maintain function. Look at what the body can do!

- **Fun and pleasure:** Using movement for enjoyment, to raise your mood and to play.

- **Remembering that we are more than our bodies:** Societal oppressions teach us to value ourselves and others based on a very narrow range of body types and appearances. Decentring this can be freeing.

- **Movement as self-care, not self-control:** We can stop monitoring and regulating our bodies. Instead, we can eat and move because it feels good.

As we liberate ourselves from oppressive societal messages, this liberation spreads outwards to our friend groups and our larger communities.

Here's this week's experiment:

- How do you feel about movement? Do oppressive societal messages ever make it hard for you to use movement in your self-care?

_____

_____

_____

_____

- Is exercise ever a punishment or compensation for eating, or a way to morph your body into societal beauty norms?

_____

_____

_____

_____

- When does physical activity feel joyful, fun or playful for you? What makes it so?

_____

_____

_____

_____

- Is movement part of your daily self-care?

_____

_____

_____

_____

SOME TINY CHUNKS TO GET YOU STARTED:

- Dancing or swaying to one favourite song

- Four minutes of Tabata (which uses twenty-second vigorous bursts, followed by ten-second rests)

- Online chair-based fitness classes or recordings

Deeper Dive

Check out an eleven-minute Couch Potato Yoga video that is fully seated and beginner friendly, taught by activist Jessamyn Stanley, who identifies as a queer, femme, plus-size woman of colour. The irreverent, fun energy she brings helps me to remember to approach movement with body neutrality. A link is available at www.farzanadoctor.com/52weeks

WEEK 36

Review and Reflection

HEY, IT'S been nine months already! In addition to reviewing the past three weeks, you might find it interesting to do another quarterly review of the Self- and Community Care Wheel (Week 3). Without grading yourself or getting perfectionistic, notice any shifts so far.

This month, we returned to the body and understanding how we can support it.

Take a few minutes to revisit and absorb this month's content, and to complete or repeat experiments that interested you. Here's a checklist of what we explored in the experiments:

PEACE Breathing

☐ Try the PEACE breathing technique once a day. Use habit stacking or a sticky note as a reminder.

Is Your Body Saying No?

☐ Use the body scan activity to notice if your body is saying no.

☐ Also notice when your body says yes.

A Body-Neutral Approach to Movement

☐ Reflect on the messages you've learned about exercise, movement and your body.

☐ Try on a body neutrality approach to movement.

MONTH
TEN

This month, we're returning
to a focus on mental
and emotional strategies.

Befriend Your Inner Critic

"I'M MY OWN worst enemy" is a common saying. Most of us have an internal critical voice that shoots us negative messages. This part of ourselves can feel difficult and confusing.

For example, when it comes to self-care, I have a cheerleader part that is all, "Yay, you can do it! Good for you!" and another part that says, "You won't be able to keep this up, you know. Eventually you'll forget. Anyway, this is booooring."

You would think that we should affirm the cheerleader and ignore or battle the part that sounds self-defeating or self-sabotaging. But there's a better way. We can befriend each part and recognize their important functions.

Internal Family Systems theory in a nutshell

Parts work, which in recent years has been popularized by the work of Dr. Richard Schwartz, who developed Internal Family Systems Theory (IFS), is a framework that is useful for understanding the varying—and sometimes seemingly opposing—parts of ourselves.

IFS reframes the inner critic as an internal "manager" whose function is to protect us—from humiliation, disappointment or other difficult feelings. Sometimes it sounds like a mean teacher or disapproving parent. Most inner critics developed in childhood, so the inner critic can also feel and sound like a scared child.

Like the homeostatic impulse (Week 6), the inner critic wants to stop you in your tracks to avoid discomfort. I think of the inner critic as an arm of the homeostatic impulse.

Now that we're more than three-quarters of the way through this journey, let's look at how the inner critic might be responding to self-care changes we've made. Here's an example of how it interrupts my plans to do Zumba:

"Uh oh. You're going to injure yourself! Watch your knees!!"

"You want to make this a regular thing, but like everything else, you'll probably lose interest and quit soon."

"You don't have time for this. We have a long list of to-dos waiting."

"Doesn't this look ridiculous? I hope no one is watching."

The trick is to make friends with the inner critic and recognize its *positive intention*. But first you need to get better acquainted with it.

Here's this week's experiment:

1 Pause for a moment to relax your body. Take a few deep breaths. Make your exhalations longer than your inhalations.

2 Tune in to the inner critic. You might feel it as a sensation, or hear an internal voice, or see an image. Remain curious and open.

3 **Optional:** draw your inner critic. Don't over-think this; take less than thirty seconds to sketch it. It can be a stick figure, a blob, a fantastical creature, an animal. It might remind you of someone. Mine is a stick drawing of four-year-old me.

4   Write a list of the inner critic's worst fears and criticisms about your self-care journey. If you need examples, go back and read mine. In general, inner critics tell you that you can't succeed or shouldn't try.

_____

_____

_____

_____

_____

1   Now ask the inner critic:

What's your job?

_____

_____

_____

How do you try to protect me? From what?

_____

_____

_____

What are you afraid could happen if you took a vacation from your job?

_____

_____

2   Respond with appreciation. Thank it for its service: "Oh! You're trying to protect me from _____ (examples: humiliation, disappointment and possible failure). Thanks for doing that."

_____

_____

_____

3   Try a compassionate, validating statement: "Yeah, it's true _____ can be challenging. And maybe _____ will happen (examples: people will make fun of me, I'll get injured, I'll feel bad)."

_____

_____

_____

4   Remind the inner critic that you can handle it:

"I'm a grown-up now and I have people, resources and strategies to support me today, even when scary things happen."

"I might not have had that help when I was small, but I do now. I can take the risk today."

5   Notice if the inner critic relaxes a bit.

> **TIPS** Sometimes parts that hold our wounds (known as "exiles" in IFS theory) come to the surface to share their pain when the inner critic takes a rest. For example, my young self, who loved to sing and dance around the house, needed to talk about how crestfallen she felt when she was told to stop. If this happens, hold space the way you would for any beloved child. It might be easier to dialogue on paper or with the help of a friend or therapist.

Deeper Dive

To learn more about IFS, see www.farzanadoctor.com/52weeks for:

- A link to a five-minute conversation between Esther Perel and Richard Schwartz. They talk about using IFS to heal wounds that drive the inner critic's protective impulse.

- A link to a seven-minute guided meditation by psychotherapist Ekta Hattangady that helps the listener connect with the inner child.

WEEK 38

Fail More

WHAT DID you fail at this week?

If you're like me, that question induces cringe.

Most of us have learned that mistakes and failures are embarrassing, or worse—that they could lead to harsh criticism, unfair blame or punishment from authority figures. And as we know, everything is structural, so marginalization plays a big role in how our mistakes and failures are perceived and responded to; marginalized people, in general, are treated with far more suspicion and scrutiny than those with more privilege.

On an individual and community level, we need to shift our perceptions. We must encourage one another to fail more.

A sidenote about shame versus guilt

Shame is about finding fault or flaw with *who I am*.

Guilt is finding fault or flaw in *what I did*.

Guilt is considered to be adaptive and self-corrective, while shame is not. However, guilt is sometimes unwarranted and learned.

When you feel guilt, ask yourself if your behaviour was truly harmful. For example, if you feel guilty for saying no or taking a break, might that be unwarranted or learned? Are you actually harming anyone?

So what did you fail at this week? I'll go first.

Remember that example I gave about habit stacking in Week 22? My goal was to add more fruit after meals to neuroplastically create a new habit cue.

Well, that worked for a few days, then I failed. Then I started again for a few days. And failed. And so on. Every single time I've gone back to edit this book, Week 22 makes me squirm a little. Failing feels terrible.

But what if we could reframe failure as *not trying* in the first place? As *learning*? What if we believed that failure is *a teacher*?

We'd likely take more risks, make more mistakes, gain wisdom and be more self-compassionate.

My reframe could sound like:

> I've tried the fruit strategy about fifty times. Hey, that's a lot of trying! I'm glad I tried. It worked about half the time, which was a 50% improvement. That's pretty good.
>
> I can continue doing it this way, accepting this outcome as good enough (or success!), or reassess and try something new. Or I can seek guidance from someone more experienced with gentle nutrition (see Week 22). I'll have to try (and fail) some more!

Note, this is *process-oriented* thinking, which values the learning and small changes and isn't focussed on a perfectionistic end result.

Okay, your turn. What did you fail at this week?

Here's this week's experiment:

- Reflect on one thing you failed at this week. Can you reframe the failure? Did your effort teach you something new? Consider doing this with a loved one or your work, volunteer or activist teams so that you can help one another shift your views and group norms about failure.

_____

_____

_____

TIPS If you were punished or criticized for making mistakes, you may need to attend to the feelings that arise from that. Try PEACE breathing (Week 33) or tune in to your Window of Capacity (Week 14) and use somatic resourcing (Week 15) to help with any difficult feelings that may come up. Talk with a loved one or counsellor.

WEEK 39

Do Less

OVER THE last couple of years, "quiet quitting" has entered our mainstream lexicon. This term refers to intentionally reducing engagement at work. It might look like refusing to work beyond the job's description and hours. In some cases it means doing the bare minimum. There is a range of motivation for quiet quitting, including dissatisfaction with the job and a desire to prioritize well-being.

According to Gallup, this trend gained popularity in 2021, and it's estimated that at least 50% of the US workforce is less engaged at work than before.

No surprise, right? The pandemic—a chronic stress situation—has had an unprecedented impact on us. Uncertainty, loss, illness and understaffing tired us out and continue to do so. And perhaps people were *already* tired by overwork, underfunding, inequities and vicarious trauma.

More than ever, I heard friends, colleagues and clients pausing to ask big questions like: Do I still want to do this work? Can I work less? Do my values align with this organization? Do I like working from home? Where do I want to live?

Might there be wisdom in quiet quitting? And could we channel the best parts of it into self- and community care?

Take a moment to consider how you feel about these examples:

- A burnt-out teacher, after much discussion, and after processing feelings of guilt, internalized capitalism and ableism, takes a long-term disability leave to recover.

- A physiotherapist who'd normally say yes to requests to join various workplace committees takes a risk and tells her supervisor that she won't be attending them for at least a year. This gives her an additional two hours per week that she uses for breaks.

- A hospital worker begins using her sick time, even when not sick. She'd previously worked through pain and illness and had built up a lot of sick time.

- A mental health counsellor normally offers sixty-minute counselling appointments. But their workload is so high that they often have to stay late at the office completing administrative tasks. Instead, they let clients know that due to volume, sessions will need to be forty-five minutes. They do this without their supervisor's pre-approval because in the past, she's been unsupportive.

- A refugee and immigration lawyer creates an out-of-office email notification letting clients know that it may take longer for her to get back to them. In the process of doing this, she realizes that she'd been responding to every email as though it was urgent rather than triaging them.

- A chaplain identifies that the population he's working with is triggering his childhood trauma. He quits the job and finds one that involves less countertransference.

- A caregiver who is taking care of a close relative has a Zoom meeting with other family members and lets them know she is exhausted. She feels guilty doing this because she loves her relative and has believed she should do this work selflessly. The meeting results in others pitching in with visits and by paying for food delivery and home maintenance.

- A volunteer at a dog shelter notices that the role is not what he expected. He feels depleted after each shift. He leaves and investigates other places he might volunteer.

- An activist resigns from an advisory committee role that she doesn't enjoy and switches to other activist roles she likes more. This was me! It was a revelation to understand that activism could be enjoyable.

Here's this week's experiment:

- Reflect on the above examples. Notice your reactions. If there was discomfort or excitement, tune into whether any of the examples resonate with your situation or needs.

- Are there ways you could practise doing less in service of your well-being? What risks and obstacles might you encounter in doing so? What support might you need?

- How might you support your loved ones, co-workers or activist friends if they decide to do the same?

Doing less and community care

When we model doing less in service of our well-being, it can have a ripple effect, offering others permission to do the same. Together, we can shift our work cultures to be gentler, slower and more nurturing.

Review and Reflection

LOOK AT you! It's been almost ten months! These last three weeks focussed on mental and emotional strategies to address self-care and community care.

Take a few minutes to revisit and absorb this month's content, and to complete or repeat experiments that interested you. Here's a checklist of what we explored in the experiments:

Befriend Your Inner Critic

☐ Give the inner critic exercise a try.

Fail More

☐ Reflect on one thing you failed at this week. Consider reframing failure. Try this with others to shift group norms about failure.

Do Less

☐ Reflect on the "doing less" anecdotes.

☐ Consider if there are ways you could practise doing less in service of your well-being. Identify and address any risks and obstacles as well as the support you'll need. Think about how you can support others to do the same.

MONTH
ELEVEN

This month, we return to the
body and strategies to support it.

WEEK 41

Water

HAVE YOU been hydrating enough? My friends, colleagues and clients tell me that they often forget to drink water. I think we sometimes neglect our thirst (and other bodily sensations) when we are hyper- or hypo-aroused (Week 14).

Water intake impacts our mood. A 2014 French study looked at the impact of hydration on mood and physiological sensations. The researchers increased the amount of water that "low drinkers" (people who drank less than 1.2 litres per day) consumed to 2.5 litres per day and saw an improvement in mood. They also decreased the volume of the "high drinkers" (people who drank 2–4 litres per day) to 1 litre per day and saw a detrimental effect on mood and feelings of calm (if you'd like to learn more, see www.farzanadoctor.com/52weeks for a link to the study).

Let's pause here and fill our glasses, shall we? (No really, take a sip!)

Need to find ways to drink more water? Here are some hacks:

- Start your day with two glasses of water. I start with the glass on my bedside table, and then refill it, adding a squeeze of lemon. I started this habit years ago, habit stacking (Week 22) it to waking up, and the repetition neuroplastically made it stick (Week 5).

- Refill your bottle or cup as soon as you empty it so it's easy to grab.

- Track your consumption with an app or in a journal. Or try something fun like putting eight dimes (or other light objects) in your left pocket and transferring them to your right pocket each time you drink another cup of water.

- If you need help, ask your loved ones or workmates to remind you to drink more water.

- Don't like the taste of water or find it boring? Vary your drinks with non-caffeinated teas, or add ice, mint leaves, berries or slices of cucumber or orange. Put out jugs of these in common areas to encourage workmates or loved ones to join you.

Here's this week's experiment:

- Notice how much you drink each day and if you're not getting enough, consider trying one of the strategies listed above.

_____

_____

_____

_____

_____

WEEK 42

Sleep

IF YOUR caregivers were fairly resourced and organized, you probably had a sleep routine when you were a kid.

Here's what I recall from my childhood:

- There was a five-minute warning for getting ready for bed ("When this TV show is done, upstairs!")

- Then we were sent up (usually with grumbling) to brush our teeth, wash our faces and change into pyjamas.

- Next there'd be stories or, when we were old enough, time for reading on our own.

- Then lights out.

These steps helped my mind to communicate to my body (and my parents to me) that it was time to shut down for the day.

You may have had a different experience. Perhaps consistent pre-sleep routines never existed because caregivers didn't know how to offer or enforce them. Maybe bedtime was scary or unpredictable in childhood; for example, if there was abuse (or witnessing of abuse), arguing adults or other chaos at night.

I lost my consistent sleep routine after my mother died. With no one monitoring me, I read novels late into the night, and fiction was a solace for my grief.

As adults, it's common for stress and traumas to knock us off pre-sleep routines and we may have trouble falling asleep or staying asleep. Helper and activist types might find themselves mulling over the tense or fraught contents of their day when they are trying to fall asleep or having cortisol spikes that cause middle-of-the-night rousing.

Experts call a pre-sleep routine that encourages good sleep "sleep hygiene," a clinical and, in my opinion, rather unmotivating term. I prefer to think of it as "putting myself to bed."

Some of the steps for putting ourselves to bed might include:

- Setting an intention to have a sleep routine (see Week 23)

- Beginning an hour before bedtime, dimming lights and screens

- Avoiding or reducing food and drink that will bother our sleep (e.g., heavy or spicy food before bed, caffeine, alcohol)

- Taking a bath before bed to relax

- Listening to a guided sleep meditation (see Week 49) or self-hypnosis (see Week 50)

- Using a journal to record gratitude or self-compassion, release worries or acknowledge and let go of any vicarious trauma residue (see Week 11)

- Listening to calming music or reading a book

- Light stretching, pre-sleep yoga, self-shiatsu, self-massage or sex

- Saying goodnight to someone in person, or by phone or text

- Mouth taping, where you place a one-centimetre piece of tape over your lips to train yourself to breathe through your nose (more on this next week)

Here's this week's experiment:

- Notice your current sleep routine. Could it use some help?

_____

_____

_____

_____

_____

- Try on one of the above pre-sleep activities.

_____

_____

_____

_____

_____

- Rate your sleep after trying a new pre-sleep activity.

_____

_____

_____

_____

_____

Deeper Dive

See www.farzanadoctor.com/52weeks for a link to "Wee Hours Rescue," a six-minute meditation by Mary Maddux. Maddux's recording is my go-to guided meditation for when I wake up in the middle of the night from a bad dream or hot flash and have trouble falling back to sleep. By using guided meditations such as this, we can shift our emotional responses to disturbed sleep.

WEEK 43
Take a Breath

WE SHOULDN'T have to think about how we breathe, right? Well, it's true that breathing is an automatic subconscious physical function, but we can experience big benefits from being conscious about how we do it.

Have you ever noticed that you breathe more shallowly when you're stressed? Recall that when we are out of our Window of Capacity (Week 14), in a state of overwhelm, we might even hold our breath. This continues the stress response.

Linda Stone first coined the term "email apnea," which describes breath-holding, or shallow breathing, while reading email. This might be because email—its content and volume—can be overwhelming. For some, email apnea is a habitual pattern.

Another stressed breathing habit is breathing too quickly with our mouths open, which can trigger hyper-arousal. Learning simple techniques for breathing more calmly and slowly can reduce stress levels (Week 15). Here are three that I like:

- Doubling exhalations. For example: breathing in for a count of three and exhaling for a count of six is a simple exercise I've mentioned in earlier chapters.

- While breathing, sensing into the diaphragm, ribs and lungs. Don't try to do it "right," just notice, and feel into your body.

- Five-finger meditation. Slowly trace your left hand with your right (reverse this if you're left-handed), as though tracing mountains and valleys. Inhale as your finger traces upward, then exhale as it moves downward.

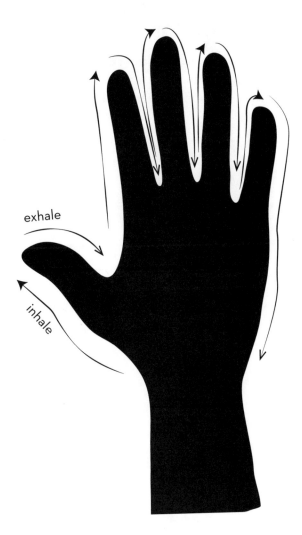

exhale

inhale

In Week 42, I mentioned mouth taping. It's a way to train our bodies to nose breathe (instead of mouth breathing) during the day or while we sleep. It wasn't until I read *Breath* by science journalist James Nestor that I understood the range of benefits we get from shifting from mouth breathing to nose breathing. These can include: decreased anxiety, better dental health, increased athletic performance and recovery, improved cognitive function, a healthier immune system, reduced risk of snoring and sleep apnea, and better sleep quality.

Here's this week's experiment:

- Notice how you breathe when you are in front of a screen. Are you holding your breath? Now notice your breathing while doing other activities: reading a book, doing dishes, attending a meeting, eating a meal.

- Try one of the above breath techniques.

Deeper Dive

See www.farzanadoctor.com/52weeks for links to:

- a ten-minute video conversation between James Nestor and Rangan Chatterjee in which they discuss the benefits of nose breathing and mouth taping at night. I was intensely skeptical of mouth taping when I first heard about it, but the science is compelling.

- a six-minute video about calm breathing from my sister, Fariya Doctor, who is a certified Buteyko instructor and Feldenkrais practitioner.

If you'd like to learn more about breathing, read James Nestor's book *Breath*.

Review and Reflection

THIS MONTH we returned to body-based strategies. Take a few minutes to revisit and absorb the content, and to complete or repeat experiments that interested you. Here's a checklist of what we explored in this month's experiments:

Water

☐ Notice how much you drink each day and if you're not getting enough, scan the list of strategies.

Sleep

☐ Think about your current sleep routine and whether it could use some tweaks. If so, try one or more of the strategies that appeal to you.

Take a Breath

☐ Pay attention to how you breathe while doing a variety of activities.

☐ Try out one of the techniques to breathe more slowly and calmly.

MONTH
TWELVE

This month, our focus
is on our online habits.

WEEK 45

Reflecting on Our Online Lives

MANY OF us spend hours online every day, responding to messages, checking social media and news sites, playing games or dating. By reflecting on our online life, we can be more mindful and intentional.

One way to reflect is to notice how your online habits have changed over time. Doing this helps me to understand how I can be less reactive and more responsive. It makes me question expectations around availability and response times.

I'm old enough to remember a time before email, the internet and smart phones were ubiquitous. When I was in my twenties, my work, including checking phone messages (and later email, which became more available in my late twenties), was restricted to my shifts. Back then, activist meetings were scheduled in person at each gathering. Sometimes (okay, I'm really dating myself here) we used phone trees to get a message out.

I joined Facebook in my thirties, when I was getting ready to publish my first novel. It expanded my literary world, made it easier to spread the word about events and I found the platform fun.

In my forties, I online dated for a few years. I appreciated the way it opened doors to people I'd never have met through my own social circles. In general, it was a great experience. But I did sometimes feel preoccupied by ghosting, creepy messages and insecurity. I know I'm not alone.

Now in my early fifties, I'm on five different social media platforms; I use them for book marketing, entertainment and for connection to my communities. I learn about activist campaigns and literary events, and I meet new colleagues and allies. I love that my phone allows me to send messages, photos and videos immediately and globally. But sometimes all the messaging apps and social media inboxes (why are there so many?) are distracting and overwhelming, or I get caught up in a post's likes and comments, and worse, the presence of meanness and trolls. As new messaging apps and social media platforms recede or emerge, I'm pausing to think about which I need and want. Frankly, I enjoy them less than I used to.

Even when I silence notifications, I can feel an impulse to respond immediately. I blame this on our collective internalized capitalism (Week 9). More and more, I'm questioning our culture's push for immediacy and 24-7 availability.

In 2022, following Portugal, France and Spain, the Ontario government passed legislation requiring employers with twenty-five or more employees to create right-to-disconnect policies. This gives workers the right to disconnect from emails, phones, video calls and other communications at the end of their workday. The federal government may follow suit. I hope laws like these promote a social norm of not working during time off.

Perhaps all of us can promote the right to disconnect in our activist, friend, volunteer and work groups by being mindful of our expectations and encouraging others to slow their response times.

Here's this week's experiment:

- Take stock of your history of online habits, reviewing your use of social media, gaming and dating platforms as well as messaging apps and email. In the next two weeks, we'll address specific strategies for tweaking email, social media and dating app use.

_____

_____

_____

_____

- Start a conversation about this in your circles.

Deeper Dive

Are you addicted to your phone? I know that I can easily slip into phone habits that include doomscrolling and repetitive checking for messages. I often have to remind myself to put my phone down and experience the world mindfully. If you're curious about phone addiction, see www.farzanadoctor.com/52weeks for a phone use quiz by Sharon Horwood at Deakin University in Australia.

WEEK 46

I Hate Email

OKAY, I don't hate email, but it can stress me out, and I've definitely experienced email apnea (see Week 43).

So I took stock of my inbox.

There was outdated clutter: a self-help newsletter I'd subscribed to a long time ago but no longer read, offers of 20% off new dresses from a website I'd scanned three years ago, and an appeal from a charity I once supported.

There was repetition between social media and email from organizations that duplicate messages across platforms. During elections, there are unsolicited appeals, including from parties I don't support, and even from the US, where I do not live.

Besides the problem of volume, I was responding to everything in a reactive way, rather than structuring my email time. This often interrupted my writing time. Like every other aspect of my life, I needed to consider my boundaries.

How about you? How do you feel about your inbox? If it's all good, skip ahead. If not, try this week's experiments.

Here's this week's experiment:

Try at least two of the following:

- Notice which groups send messages that you also see on social media. Choose one platform through which they can communicate with you and stay subscribed there.

- Unsubscribe to at least one auto-generated email you don't want. Ahhh! Wasn't that satisfying? If you don't want to deal with unsubscribes manually, there are apps that can help with this, such as Unroll.me.

- Schedule your inbox time to avoid constant checking. Use a timer.

- Consider creating folders. I have separate ones for my activist group, client payments and electronic receipts I'll need at tax time, which makes it easier to find what I'm looking for.

- Learn about your email program's features. For example, I'm a fan of Gmail's snooze, star, smart compose and label functions. I also use the schedule function for non-urgent emails so they arrive during a person's workday rather than on the weekend or at night.

- Other strategies for structuring your email time:

  - Auto-saving email addresses

  - Creating auto replies and out-of-office messages

  - Writing auto signatures

  - Creating templates for frequent types of emails to save time

Groups and email

- Initiate a conversation among your groups to check in about emails. Together, set guidelines that make it easier and better for all. For example:

  - Set a rule to stop using email to schedule meetings to cut out a lot of unnecessary back and forth. Use scheduling apps instead.

  - Avoid reply all and unnecessary cc'ing.

  - The shelter I volunteer at created a weekly one-page newsletter rather than sending out bits of information in multiple emails.

WEEK 47

Mindful Online Engagement

FOR ME, the hardest part of online interactions is managing my time, emotions and energy. When I completed the phone addiction quiz, it was clear that I needed to figure out how to be more intentional and less reactive. If I didn't, checking my phone would continue to feel compulsive and time-sucking, and have a negative impact on my mood.

Here are some strategies I like that bring more mindfulness to the experience:

- Set time limits to avoid travelling down too many rabbit holes. Use alarms if necessary.

- Schedule time for responding to notifications or messages so they don't interfere with or distract you from other tasks or activities. Create online office hours so others know when it's best to contact you.

- Alternatively, schedule time for your deep thinking work and silence notifications and ringers during that time.

- Reduce urgency by asking yourself, "Can this wait until later?" (In my experience, it nearly always can wait.) This also gives me time to think about my boundaries (Weeks 17 and 18) before replying to requests.

- Before checking social media or a dating app, consider filling yourself with compassion and curiosity. It will help you to be less easily knocked over by emotions such self-doubt, comparison and jealousy.

- Curate your feeds so they bring you more of what you want. Need reminders about a self-care strategy you've been trying? Want to learn more about a topic? Need some mood elevators (Week 26)? Follow the hashtags, find your favourite people and be part of communities that take you in these directions. Block or unfollow the rest.

Intentional breaks from platforms and apps can also be useful. Some ideas:

- Schedule time off, starting small and working up. An hour before bed, for example, or a phone-free dinner, Social Media–free Saturday or Dating App–free Wednesday, or a post-free vacation.

- Alternatively, consider reframing this exercise with an additive approach. What will you do instead of being online? More bedtime reading? A Saturday picnic or trip? A Wednesday hangout with friends?

- If you don't meet your goal, be kind to yourself. See if you can treat failure as a good attempt (see Week 38) and a learning experience.

Here's this week's experiment:

- This week, try at least one of the ideas above.

  - During a break, notice if you focus on life a little differently (experiencing versus recording and documenting). What did you do instead?

  _____

  _____

  _____

  _____

  - When ending a break, consider how you might engage differently once you're back. For example, are there groups or accounts you might unfollow?

  _____

  _____

  _____

  _____

- Invite others to join you in your intentionality and breaks so you can support one another with this experiment.

TIPS If you worry about getting FOMO (fear of missing out) during a break, let a few friends know in advance so that they know to contact you in other ways. I often tell people that I'm going to take a break. The external accountability helps me.

Deeper Dive

Okay, this is more fun than deep, but check out www.farzanadoctor.com/52weeks for a link to a three-minute *Baroness von Sketch* episode about LinkedIn notifications.

WEEK 48
Review and Reflection

CONGRATS ON getting to Week 48! You're close to finishing this book. Time to celebrate by posting your achievement on social media. (Just kidding! Well, actually, you could try to do that mindfully.)

Take a few minutes to revisit and absorb the content, which focussed on our online lives. Flip back to complete or repeat experiments that interested you. Here's a checklist of what we explored in this month's experiments:

Reflecting on Our Online Lives

☐ Take stock of your history of online habits, reviewing your use of social media, gaming and dating platforms as well as messaging apps and email.

☐ Start a conversation about this in your circles.

I Hate Email

☐ Try some of the suggested strategies to wrangle your email.

Mindful Online Engagement

☐ Consider if you can bring more mindfulness to your online life.

☐ Take a break (of any duration) and notice how you feel.

☐ Invite others to join you in your intentionality and breaks for mutual support.

MONTH
THIRTEEN

In this last month, we wrap things up
with strategies for mind, body and spirit.

WEEK 49
Surrender

THIS MORNING I awoke to the room spinning. This is benign paroxysmal positional vertigo, an unpredictable dizziness that hits me a couple of times a year. I got out of bed, did the Foster manoeuvre (a weird half-somersault technique) to treat it, and returned to bed, still a little dizzy.

BPPV arrives without much rhyme or reason. One night, after exhausting myself with a web search on BPPV (mostly unhelpful medical rabbit holes and a repetition of what my doctor has told me), I switched course and typed: spiritual meaning of BPPV. Why not? Nothing else was helping much. I read: dizziness suggests a need for surrender.

As an over-functioner (see Week 10), someone who reacts to stress by trying to control the heck out of things, this is *never* bad advice for me.

As I've mentioned in previous weeks, over-functioning is a common coping strategy and sometimes a trauma response. For me, it feels like anxiety or hyper-arousal. Likewise, under-functioning can be a hint I'm in hypo-arousal (Week 14).

> A caveat—if you really do need to *act* to solve an issue (for example, to get yourself checked out by your doctor, or ensure your safety), remember to do that first, before surrendering and accepting!

What does surrender mean? It means acknowledging the overwhelm and just . . . letting what's happening . . . happen.

And so I lay down on my back on the floor. I surrendered to the dizziness.

In the stillness, I remembered that I'd been feeling some intense body image negativity that week, spending way too much energy figuring out what to wear to an upcoming event. I'd been scrolling through online clothing stores, adding things to baskets, but in the end, not buying anything because nothing seemed right.

So I surrendered again.

I thought about my dog Maggie, who'd died a year earlier. A wave of grief arrived, and I surrendered to that and cried for a bit. And then I daydreamed a little. Then I thought about how Maggie didn't care about my body image issues and probably enjoyed my body's softness. I doubt she was preoccupied about her own ageing body's new lumps and bumps. I imagined her putting her head on my belly. I laughed, love filling my body. I surrendered like only a dog knows how.

The BPPV persisted for a few more hours, and then, as it always does for me, mysteriously left again.

Here's this week's experiment:

When feeling overwhelmed or having non-urgent physical symptoms, try this out.

- Relax your body and imagine surrendering to the sensations and feelings. What comes up? Notice if this rest restores you, brings new awareness, helps you find a way through an issue, or perhaps lights the path to a previously unfindable solution.

_____

_____

_____

_____

_____

_____

- Note that your stress might be linked to something personal (as in the above example), or a larger community or societal issue (I've also used this exercise when overwhelmed by our global climate crisis).

Deeper Dive

See www.farzanadoctor.com/52weeks for a beautiful guided meditation by Sarah Blondin on learning to surrender.

TIPS Guided meditations are helpful when you need help steering your mind toward calmer waters. You can find thousands on YouTube or on apps such as Insight Timer. Find a recording with a voice you enjoy and find calming. You can also record your own customized guided meditations and include reminders and affirmations that are especially helpful to you. Group meditations, where there is a sense of community or collective synchrony and flow, can be fun and powerful too. Consider joining a group or inviting others to join you.

WEEK 50
Self-Hypnosis

WHEN MY mother was dying of cancer, a family friend referred her to Bob Proctor, who, back in 1982, lived near us.

He wasn't Oprah-level famous yet, and none of us knew anything about his methods, and certainly nothing about hypnosis. He sat at our dining room table and talked to us, preacher style, about healing. At eleven years old, I felt both fascinated by and skeptical about his hopefulness.

I think the goal of their subsequent one-on-one sessions was to cure her. What I recall was how he seemed to help her calmly face her illness, and later, her death.

Bob gave a self-hypnosis cassette to my sister, who was dealing with her own grief and adolescent stress. I "borrowed" it and listened to it for years until the tape wore out and snapped. I can still recall how it began, "Just listen to my voice, you hear nothing but my voice, let your eyes go closed, let your eyelids relax..." It ended up being an important resource for me during my tween and teen years.

Years later, as a psychotherapist, I learned how to provide hypnotherapy, and it's one of my favourite tools. I also use self-hypnosis when I'm anxious or having trouble sleeping. It's a useful strategy for slowing down and surrendering (see last week) instead of over-functioning or over-controlling situations in times of stress.

What is hypnosis?

Forget what you might have learned from stage shows and pop culture. "Quack like a chicken" is neither respectful nor therapeutic.

Hypnosis is a normal state of focussed or absorbed attention. It can feel like a deeply relaxed state, where one's sense of possibilities opens up and ego defences lower. It works on a subconscious level and can bypass the homeostatic impulse and inner critic (Weeks 6 and 37).

During hypnosis, the practitioner can offer suggestions (e.g., for deep sleep, smoking cessation, well-being, pain management). Research indicates that it can be helpful in addressing a number of psychological issues and concerns.

Here's this week's experiment:

- Consider trying a self-hypnosis recording. Search online for one that will address your unique concern or self-care goal, for example "self-hypnosis for sleep" or "self-hypnosis for anxiety."

- Remember to be in a place where you can be undisturbed, and of course, when you are not operating machinery.

- Like with guided meditations, there are thousands of free recordings on YouTube or on apps such as Insight Timer. Sample them in advance so you find one with a voice that suits you. You can find a few that I like at www.farzanadoctor.com/52weeks.

WEEK 51

Recharge

WE NEED rest. But we also need to recharge. This is especially true for recovering from or preventing burnout.

Our energy levels are a little like smart phone batteries.

If the battery is at 5%, and we don't have access to the charger, it's best to not use the phone in order to avoid depleting the battery. And then, when we can plug in, we recharge.

Similarly, if we're depleted, we just have to stop what we're doing and rest. After, we need recharging activities.

How do we recharge? Each of us is different.

Take a minute right now to close your eyes and remember a moment that uplifted you, made you smile, or left you with a feeling of delight, awe or energy in your body.

Next, jot down what came up. Think of another moment and write that down. Keep going until you have a list of at least three or more things.

Here's what I came up with. Moments that included:

- Novelty—checking out a new place in my neighbourhood or farther away, or engaging in new learning or even trying a new recipe or restaurant

- Connection—a conversation, text, walk or dinner with a friend

- Affection and touch—hugging my partner or petting an animal

- Spiritual connection or awe—a walk in nature, engaging in group prayer, pulling a tarot card, grabbing a random book from my shelf and reading a page

- Movement—turning on a random song in my phone's playlist and swaying or dancing to it

- Spontaneity—an unexpected, unplanned moment such as a last-minute hangout with a friend or turning a corner and discovering a beautiful mural

- Meaningful activity—service work, volunteering, attending a rally or solidarity event

- Looking forward to something—planning a gathering, a vacation, an outing

Here's this week's experiment:

- Create your own list of recharging activities. Post it somewhere you'll see it. Do one or two of them this week. Did they charge your battery?

_____

_____

_____

- Ask yourself: What's it like to intentionally add these activities to your life? Does it feel easy? Does it seem frivolous? Is it sometimes hard to give yourself permission?

_____

_____

_____

- How might you share the joy and invite others into it?

_____

_____

_____

_____

TIPS Some of the things on the list might be easy to accomplish and some will require planning and money. Ensure you have a mix.

WEEK 52

Review and Reflection

WHAT? IT'S been a whole year!

Take a few minutes to revisit and absorb this last month's content, and to complete or repeat experiments that interested you. Here's a checklist of what we explored in the experiments:

Surrender

☐ If you're stressed or overwhelmed by a personal, community or societal issue, try surrendering to it. Notice if this rest helps you find a way through the issue, or perhaps brings you a previously unfindable solution.

Self-Hypnosis

☐ Try a self-hypnosis recording to help you with your self- and community care goals.

Recharge

☐ Create a list of recharging activities and try one or two of them.

☐ Consider how you might share the joy and invite others to join you.

And an extra reflection:

- *Congratulations!* You finished the year! How do you feel?

_____

_____

_____

_____

_____

_____

_____

_____

_____

- Which weeks stand out for you (they might have stood out for being interesting, difficult, annoying, helpful, etc.)?

_____

_____

_____

_____

_____

_____

_____

_____

_____

_____

_____

- Have a look at your Self- and Community Care Wheel from Week 3. Non-judgmentally notice if any shifts have occurred.

_____

_____

_____

_____

_____

_____

_____

_____

_____

So what's next?

WHILE THIS book contains forty hacks and other good ideas, it's not exhaustive. And it can't be—there are as many self- and community care strategies as there are humans, and we each need to find the ones that work best for us. I know that as I edited this book, I added and subtracted, trying to hone which concepts seemed most important to me. A year from now, I'm sure I'll want to add and subtract some more (I'm reminding my inner critic that nothing is perfect or needs to be).

Perhaps some of these ideas piqued your curiosity and you want to go on a few deeper dives on your own. Maybe a new class? A group? Another book?

Our self- and community care practices are not linear or constant. They ebb and flow over time depending on life circumstances, and sometimes we need a refresher. Each time I came back to edit this guide, I found a new and helpful reminder. You might want to revisit this book from time to time.

Here are some ideas on how to keep working with this book if you'd like to do that:

- Each week, return to an idea that interested you.

- Flip randomly through the book to revisit a chapter.

- Bookmark the pages you'd like to explore further in the future.

- Start again, in the same order, and see what new insights come your way.

- Start again, in the same order, but this time with friends or work mates and see what it's like to do this with company.

Thank you for joining me on this journey. I hope it deepened your wellness and made self- and community care just a little bit easier. And sweeter.

Epilogue

SINCE I started writing this book, life changed, yet again, as it does.

One of these changes, as I mentioned in earlier chapters, was that my fourteen-year-old dog Maggie died. A new grief took over and for a while I needed to leave enough time and space around me for it to settle and integrate. I needed to pull on my own skills and the support of my community. Recovery happened through rest, talking with friends, reading kids' books about pet loss (they are so great at getting straight to the heart of the matter) and expressing my feelings through writing.

I also realized that while I didn't want the full-time responsibility of another dog, I did want to be around dogs, and that's how I started volunteering at a local dog shelter. This feels like part grief healing, part new hobby and part community service. It brings with it a new bunch of nice people (many of whom are also grieving dog friends). And of course, hanging with the dogs is a joy! It's self-care and community care.

Life will always bring us new challenges that demand a renewed focus on our well-being, and we may return to old strategies or try new ones. Just as chronic COVID stress in 2021 led me to dance more, Maggie's death sent me to the dog shelter.

What's clear to me is that I will always need a focus on self- and community care to remain physically, emotionally and spiritually well.

A final note about community care

TODAY, I gave a literary talk over Zoom. Even though I've done hundreds of these events, I tend to crackle with nervous energy during them. But today I'm fostering Minnie, a six-pound, twelve-year-old mini pinscher who likes to curl up in a human's lap to rest and stay warm. So, with her snuggled against me, I performed my poetry and remained grounded.

This is the magic of dogs, but also of co-regulation.

Earlier in this book I mentioned that humans and other animals co-regulate, our nervous systems mirroring one another. Calm moods—and their opposite, overwhelm—are contagious. In other words, when Minnie snores in my lap, my own nervous system balances. After, if I go upstairs and greet my partner with a twenty-second hug while in this state, this might help him to complete a stress response cycle. He might also find himself breathing more slowly and deeply. And then he might bring this presence to a phone call with a friend, holding space more supportively. And that friend might show more consideration to her co-worker, and so on.

As we practise self-care, the care ripples out.

Thinking back over this year, did your self-care efforts impact your community?

Did others join in when you modelled something new? Did you make new connections when accessing care from others?

Our small actions (and tiny dogs) can make a big difference.

Recommended Reading

The Body Is Not an Apology: The Power of Radical Love by Sonya Renee Taylor

Burnout: The Secret to Unlocking the Stress Cycle by Amelia and Emily Nagoski

The Four Tendencies by Gretchen Rubin

When the Body Says No: The Cost of Hidden Stress by Gabor Maté

The Myth of Normal: Trauma, Illness and Healing in a Toxic Culture by Gabor Maté and Daniel Maté

Breath by James Nestor

The Brain That Changes Itself by Norman Doidge

Intuitive Eating: A Revolutionary Anti-Diet Approach by Evelyn Tribole and Elyse Resch

The Bodacious Book of Succulence by SARK

Rest: Why You Get More Done When You Work Less by Alex Soojung-Kim Pang

How to Keep House While Drowning by KC Davis

The Happiness Advantage by Shawn Achor

Rest is Resistance: A Manifesto by Tricia Hersey

The Empath's Survival Guide: Life Strategies for Sensitive People by Judith Orloff

Wired for Love by Stan Tatkin

Polysecure: Attachment, Trauma and Consensual Nonmonogamy by Jessica Fern

Deeper Dive Links

A reminder that all Deeper Dive links can be found at www.farzanadoctor.com/52weeks

Or use this handy QR code:

Conversation Guide

Here's a suggested structure for a group or book club conversation.

1   Begin with a short grounding exercise of the group's choice. A group member might lead the group through a guided meditation, a body scan, or PEACE breathing (Week 33). At www.farzanadoctor.com/52weeks you can find a recording of PEACE breathing.

2   Decide which content you plan to discuss. If your group is meeting just once, co-create a list of topics together. If your group is meeting more regularly (weekly or monthly, for example), you may wish to move through the book a week or a month at a time.

3   Depending on your group's size, you may want to go around the circle to allow each person to share their thoughts on the content and any learning that came from trying out experiments. Questions to pose to one another:

- Did the ideas resonate for you?

- Did the experiments inspire any new thoughts, feelings or actions?

- How are you doing in your self- and community care journey? Discuss any challenges or wins.

- What support might you need?

- How might self- and community care intersect in the content you are discussing today?

- Habits and making changes are recurring themes in the book. Are there any obstacles or strategies you'd like to share with the group?

- Systemic issues, for example marginalization, inequity and oppression, are also recurring subjects. Share any thoughts about how systemic issues might connect to the content the group is discussing today.

- If you went on a Deep Dive, what did you learn?

4   End with a closing exercise. This could include conscious intention-setting (Week 23), or each person could contribute one word or sentence about what they are taking from the conversation.

Acknowledgements

I AM deeply grateful to all of the writers and thinkers whose work I've referenced in this book, as well as the hundreds of clients, co-workers and community members who've taught me everything about self- and community care.

A huge thanks to beta readers Sil Hernando, Zak Greant, Jen Vasic, Natasha Steer and Zahra Bardai for your encouragement and critical feedback.

Thanks to all the folks at Douglas & McIntyre for having faith in this book. Special thanks to Anna Comfort O'Keeffe, Caroline Skelton, Setareh Ashrafologhalai, Luke Inglis, Colleen Bidner, Corina Eberle, Annie Boyar and David Marsh.

I am grateful to live by Lake Ontario on Turtle Island, which is on the traditional territory of many nations including the Mississaugas of the Credit, the Anishnabeg, the Chippewa, the Haudenosaunee and the Wendat peoples, now home to many diverse First Nations, Inuit and Métis peoples. As a settler on stolen land, I call on other settlers to support the Indigenous-led Land Back movement.

As always, thanks to all my friends, family and community who support my writing. I appreciate every little thing you do to buoy me up.

And to my partner, Reyan Naim—I have learned so much from your generous gestures of love and care.

About the Author

FARZANA DOCTOR is a Toronto-based Registered Social Worker who has been working with individuals and couples since 1993. As an activist, educator and writer, she has taught clinicians, co-written manuals for mental health providers and contributed chapters and articles about 2SLGBTQ+ issues, anti-oppression, self-care and female genital mutilation/cutting. She is the co-founder of WeSpeakOut and the End FGM Canada Network. She has written four critically acclaimed novels and a poetry collection.

Her website is farzanadoctor.com

MAY TRUONG